THE EFFECTIVE INTERPRETING SERIES

Translating from English

Carol J. Patrie

DawnSignPress
San Diego, California

The Effective Interpreting Series: Translating from English

Producer: Joe Dannis

Printed in the United States of America.

Published by DawnSignPress.

Rosetta Stone image © Copyright The British Museum. The Rosetta Stone appears throughout the series as a symbol of translation's importance to mankind. The basalt slab was discovered in July 1799 in the small Egyptian village of Rosette on the western delta of the Nile. The stone's inscription in hieroglyphic, demotic, and Greek languages led to a crucial breakthrough in research regarding Egyptian hieroglyphs. This key to "translating silent images" into a living language symbolizes the importance of accurate transmissions of messages from one language into another.

The Rosetta Stone now resides in the British Museum in London.

Cover Design: Greg Smith

ISBN: 0-915035-85-5

10   9   8   7   6   5   4   3   2   1

Attention: Schools and Distributors

Quantity discounts for schools and bookstores are available.

For information, please contact:

DAWNSIGNPRESS
6130 Nancy Ridge Drive
San Diego, CA 92121

VISIT US AT www.dawnsign.com
858-625-0600 V/TTY 858-625-2336 FAX
ORDER TOLL FREE 1-800-549-5350

For my dear Aunt Syl, for her presence
and for keeping her "two thumbs up" attitude
during the entire project.

Acknowledgments

Expressing my gratitude to those who help create the books and videos in *The Effective Interpreting Series* is my favorite part of writing each book. This book, like the others in the series, is the result of dedicated involvement of many people. Divine Providence led me to DawnSignPress and Joe Dannis. Without Joe's generous support this work would never have reached fruition. Beginning in 1995 when *The Effective Interpreting Series* was conceived and during all the subsequent years of filming the videos and preparing the manuscripts Joe has unwaveringly believed in my vision and me. Such unconditional support is most rare and deeply appreciated.

I thank Tracie Spingarn for her detailed feedback and suggestions for improvement on an earlier version of the manuscript. Melanie Metzger provided me with invaluable assistance on various parts of the manuscript, often on short notice. Earl Fleetwood's gift for analysis helped me solve some stubborn problems in conveying concepts clearly.

Many people from Dawn Sign Press contributed to this effort. Yoon Lee's gift in creating and composing video material shines through in this work. I am grateful for Joseph Josselyn's contribution to the project through his superb videoediting skills and to Dan Veltri for his valuable assistance with aspects of videoediting. I am also deeply appreciative of the contributions to the project of Ryan Stern, Wendy Staroba Loreen, and Kirsten Chrisman.

I thank Rebecca Ryan for providing the steady support and encouragement that all authors need but only very fortunate ones receive. She is gifted with a gentle and discerning eye and an insight that allows her to help me grapple with complex topics. Rebecca is a rare example of enthusiasm and grace under pressure and I am deeply grateful to her for her cheerful assistance in manuscript and video preparation that are of the highest standard.

Contents

Preface

When I became a professional interpreter in 1968, interpreter education was rare. Since that time, interpreter education has made great strides. I am pleased to share with you my 33 years of experience as an interpreter and 18 years of experience as an interpreter educator. I am one of the developers of the Master of Arts in Interpretation at Gallaudet University, where I taught interpretation from 1984 to 2000. The ideas and exercises presented in this book are the result of my work developing materials that practicing and future translators and interpreters can use in or out of the classroom.

I have found that one of the greatest problems in translator and interpreter education for signed or spoken language is a lack of materials for use in the classroom. An even more severe problem is the lack of study materials that practicing and future translators and interpreters can use on their own, either for continuing professional development or to learn new skills. Translation and interpretation are very complex and require hours of appropriate practice. Often translators and interpreters want but cannot find effective ways to improve their skills. It is my hope that with the structured materials for translating English provided in this volume, practicing and future translators and interpreters will find developing translation skills to be rewarding and effective.

The English source materials provide access to a wide variety of subjects and speakers. Each speaker presents information in an organized, yet unrehearsed fashion. The source materials contain a range of levels of difficulty in terms of topic and register. The text of each speech is transcribed.

How to Use This Workbook

This book focuses on development of translation skills using English source materials. In each unit, a brief introduction provides theoretical background information on the unit's topic and discusses the relevance of that information to translation and interpretation. The introductory material is followed by a series of exercises specifically designed to apply the theoretical concepts discussed in that unit. Each exercise has three parts. The first is to respond to the exercise material and record your answers. This allows you to create a product. The second part of the exercise is to answer the study questions. Answering the study questions allows you to examine your responses (product). The third aspect of each exercise is the follow-up. The follow-up allows you to examine the processes used to arrive at your product. Information, exercises, study questions, and follow-up procedures are provided for each of the skill units in this book. The English translation skills in this workbook are preparation, analysis, transfer, reformulation, priorities, and testing the translation.

All of the exercises (recording, answering the study questions, and doing the follow-up) in each unit may be completed as out-of-classroom work or as independent work during class time, if appropriate equipment is available. This book provides complete directions for each exercise. The directions guide you to the correct location on the accompanying videotape. Each exercise has study questions and a follow-up. The study questions help provide focus and insight into your responses to the exercises. The follow-up after each exercise is designed to increase self-awareness and is fully explained on pages 3–4. The book exercises and follow-up allow you to take responsibility for creating work (product) and to analyze and develop strategies for improvement of the processes you use to create the product. At the end of each unit there is a progress tracking sheet. Use the progress tracking sheet to indicate the date you completed the exercises and to make notes regarding your progress and also to record any questions you may have about the exercise. The tracking sheet can be used in either a quantitative or a qualitative approach. More detail on the tracking sheet is provided on pages 6–7.

Translation skills are an important step in the development of interpretation skills because the process allows more time than does simultaneous interpreting. These materials stand apart from typical translation study materials because they include videotaped source texts. Ordinarily, translation source materials are in print, not in a videotaped format. Videotaped source material can be reviewed just as a printed text can and is an appropriate addition to the field of translation materials. If you are working into a language that has a written form, you can work from the transcript provided in the workbook and write your translation in the space provided. If you are working into a signed language, it is best to videotape your translation.

In the exercises, the spoken material is transcribed so there is a written form from which to work. Although English that is spoken and later transcribed is different in form than English that is created in a written format, interpreters benefit from practicing with spontaneously spoken English because this is the form of English that interpreters work with most often. The transcript of the spoken English simply provides a more accessible way to analyze the source text. Translators-in-training will find the carefully sequenced exercises, questions, and follow-up exercises effective in developing and improving translation skills.

What You Need before Beginning the Exercises

You need specific equipment in addition to the video and book in order to get the maximum benefit from these exercises. If you are working into a written language you will need a means to record your translation, either on a computer or by hand writing. If you are working into a signed language you will need a VHS VCR with a remote control that will allow you to pause the video, a supply of blank VHS videotapes, a TV monitor, an audio recorder, blank audiotapes, and a quiet place to work. If you are working into a signed language, owning a video camera would enhance the study process and is optional.

When and Where You Should Plan to Do the Exercises

Each exercise can be done independently. You should plan to do them out of class on your own time, or in a class format if your training program has a place for you to record your work. Where you do the exercises in a classroom will depend on your instructor and the equipment available. For example, if your instructional program has a language lab that will permit you to work independently and to record your work, then you can do many of the exercises independently while on campus or in class. Your teacher may introduce the exercises to you and go over your results with you.

If you are a practicing translator or interpreter and want to work on developing your professional skills you will still need all of the equipment listed previously and may proceed at your own pace. You may wish to form a study group to provide a forum for discussing your skill-development work, both product and process.

How Many Times Should You Do the Exercises?

You can benefit from doing each exercise at least twice. When you do the exercise the first time, the material that you listen to will be "cold" or unfamiliar. The skills that you are practicing may also be new and unfamiliar. When you do the exercise the second time, the material will be "warm," or familiar, because you have read and heard it once. You will be more comfortable with the process the second time. Practicing the exercises more than once allows you to control the process you use to complete the work and improve the quality of the product you create.

The Five-Step Follow-up

The five-step follow-up is presented after each exercise.

The five parts of the follow-up are:

Step 1 **Observation**

Step 2 **Selection**

Step 3 **Analysis**

Step 4 **Assessment**

Step 5 **Action**

The purpose of the follow-up is to introduce and strengthen the concepts of self-awareness and self-confidence during translation. The five-step follow-up allows you to determine the impact on the communicative function of errors in your translation. In other books in this series, *English Skills Development* and *Cognitive Processing in English,* the emphasis is on finding the reasons for errors. According to Kussmaul (1995), finding reasons for errors is appropriate for language learning classrooms, but in the case of translation, it is more relevant to determine the *communicative function* of the error. For example, does the error distort the message or is there a "sufficient degree of precision"? In Kussmaul's approach to translation evaluation, the focus is on the translation's effect on the target reader, not on what the translator was thinking while creating the translation.

Translators and interpreters who are self-aware and self-confident can enjoy lifelong learning and continuing education opportunities in a wide variety of settings, even if a teacher or mentor is not available. The self-assessment skills used in completing the five-step follow-up lead to accountability in interpretation because they allow you to analyze both the process and the product of your work.

Accountability in translation and interpretation means that you make conscious decisions about the products and processes involved in your translations and work to see that the translations and interpretations are faithful to the original message. It means that you take responsibility when the translation is not faithful to the message and correct it. A graduate of the Master of Arts in Interpretation at Gallaudet who became very familiar with the follow-up process used here suggests that the impact of the self-assessment achieved through the five-step follow-up is unparalleled (Fleetwood, 1998). In addition to increasing accountability in translation and interpretation, the follow-up for self-assessment allows an objective analysis of the product or the processes involved in translation and interpretation.

By carefully doing each follow-up, you will learn the importance of the many components of the translation process and that each is needed for a successful translation. By being able to separate translation into its component parts and processes you can better understand where to focus your efforts for improvement. Naturally, the translation process is not a segmented event in real life, but studying it in more manageable pieces allows you to determine which parts of your work are successful attempts and which parts are less successful. More importantly, it helps you to see which parts of the translation process are under your control and which are not.

The five-step follow-up is an exciting new way to improve your awareness of your performance. All students want to know "How am I doing so far?" By putting forth the effort to complete the follow-up you will be able to answer this question yourself instead of relying on a teacher to provide all of the feedback on your work. Naturally, if you are just learning the process you will need both your own analysis of your work and your teacher's input. What was missing? What was good? What accounts for my success in the exercises? Why did I miss some aspects? The sooner you adopt an analytical view of your work, the sooner your skills become reliable. You will also feel less lost in the details of learning the very complex skill of translation; instead you will feel a certain mastery and sense of accomplishment and control over your own process.

The follow-up should be completed as soon as possible after finishing the exercises. This is important as you may be asked to explain why you chose certain answers. You will be better able to gain insight into your processes if you do the follow-up immediately after the exercises. If you are working in a group, the questions and activities in the follow-up could be used in a group discussion. Even if you are working in a group, it is important to write your answers so you can refer to them later and see how much progress you have made.

Sample Rating Systems

If you are working independently and want to score your own work you can use a rating system. Attaching number ratings to linguistic performance is somewhat arbitrary, but you may find it helpful as you track your progress. This is a sample of how the first step of the follow-up could be rated using a point system. The first step of the follow-up is Observation:

5 points = reviewed all portions of the work carefully

4 points = reviewed all portions of the work

3 points = skimmed all portions of the work

2 points = skimmed some of the work

1 point = did not follow instructions

0 points = did not do the work

You can use a different approach for the Assessment stage of the five-step follow-up. This step deals with the overall effectiveness of the communicative function. You can rate errors as:

No errors—
communicative function is well preserved = 5 points

Not serious—
error does not skew the message = 4 points

Somewhat serious—
minor skew of the message due to omission of detail = 3 points

Quite serious—
total skew of the message due to following L1 syntax = 2 points

Very serious—
total skew of the message due to comprehension problems = 1 point
(Gorman, 1998)

Another system is proposed by Dollerup (1994, p. 123). Dollerup states that translation is a "social activity" that must have a high degree of fidelity. In Dollerup's system, errors are categorized as follows:

(a) an excellent translation

(b) minor inaccuracy, but the original meaning is preserved in the target language,

(c) a distortion, but not so great that the meaning of the original cannot be grasped

(d) an incomprehensible rendering; it may confuse but it will rarely lead astray,

(e) a self-contradictory rendering which is misunderstood,

(f) a rendering which reads fluently and makes perfect sense but distorts the meaning of the original (Dollerup, 1982).

It is important to realize that not all errors carry the same weight although as Dollerup writes "In a strict sense, all errors in translation violate the trust of senders and addressees" (p.124). This means that the person who created the message (the sender) and the receiver of the message (the addressee) both trust the translator to faithfully render the message into the target language. It is possible that those relying on the translator will not detect a translation error. Trust is violated because the senders and addressees believe that the translator is rendering a faithful translation. The social impact of errors can vary and should also be taken into account. Dollerup suggests that the system above categorizes the gravity of errors but does not account for the social effect of the errors. Dollerup points out that the most serious error type

(f) is least likely to be detected and that even within categories there are still more variations. For example, a distortion that involves one word can be less serious than an error involving an entire sentence, except if the single word is crucial to the meaning of the overall text.

Progress Tracking Sheet

A progress tracking sheet is at the end of each unit. This sheet is designed to help you keep track of which exercises you have completed and how well you have done on these exercises. After performing the exercise, answering the study questions, and doing the follow-up, you should fill in the tracking sheet. Note the date that you completed the exercise and give an indication of your level of accomplishment. You can use either a quantitative or a qualitative approach to track your progress. The sample chart that follows provides examples of how to note your progress using the quantitative or qualitative approach.

A quantitative approach uses a point scale. Assigning points to linguistic exercises is arbitrary, but in academic environments you may find the point system more suitable than the qualitative approach. Each of the two trials on the performance, each study question, and follow-up step can be assigned a point value. A 0 indicates that the question was not answered and a 5 indicates a full and complete response. Add the scores in each column (not row) and divide by the number of exercises to obtain a percentage for first performance, second performance, study questions, and follow-up. It is important to have separate percentages for each of these columns because the scores in the study question and follow-up columns represent different skills. The two performance columns both measure performance, but a second attempt on the same material is considered practice on "warm" or familiar material and should be weighted less heavily than the "cold" or unfamiliar first attempt.

Here is an example of a scale you can use to assign points to your work: excellent (no serious errors) = 5 points, good (some errors, but not serious) = 4 points, fair (many errors, some serious) = 3 points, not satisfactory (many errors, most are serious) = 2 points, poor (missed the point of the exercise - must redo) = 1 point.

A qualitative approach is well suited to those who are studying the material in an independent fashion or those who do not want to attach numbers and percentages to their work. In a qualitative approach you describe your response to your work rather than assigning numbers. Write down enough information to remind yourself of your level of achievement in the performance of the exercises, study questions, and follow-up.

Exercise Number	Date	First Performance	Study Questions	Follow-up Activity	Questions and Reminders	Date	Second Performance
Exercise 1 Quantitative	10/3	35/50 = 70%	20/25 = 80%	20/25 = 80%		11/5	45/50 = 90%
Qualitative		I added information not in the source text.	Able to answer questions 1–4 but not number 5	Analysis area needs work.	More careful analysis will help gauge time needed.		Translation process much easier second time.
Exercise 2 Quantitative	10/9	40/50 = 80%	20/25 = 80%	25/25 = 100%		11/15	45/50 = 90%
Qualitative		Did not add information, but omitted some detail. Difficulty with classifiers.	Similarity and difference in meaning is clearer. Better at estimating time. Competence in L2 not good.	Analysis is more accurate.	Need help with classifiers for people and bikes		Added some detail. Better overall.
Exercise 3 Quantitative	10/15	35/50 = 70%	25/25 = 100%	25/25 = 100%		11/21	45/50 = 90%
Qualitative		Very difficult passage. Errors in comprehension and estimating time needed.	Pleased with my grasp of material.	Satisfied with my progress in reviewing and analyzing work.	Understanding of material is stronger than my ability in translation performance.		Translation more faithful. I had a better idea how much time was needed.
Quantitative Totals		73%	86%	93%			90%

Introduction to Translating from English

Translation is a very old science. One of the earliest written translations in existence that we know of is the Rosetta stone. This stone tablet is inscribed with a text commemorating the official coronation of Ptolemy V as king of Egypt in 197 BC. The Egyptian priesthood published the decree that forms the trilingual inscription on the Rosetta Stone (Online Encyclopedia 2001). The same text is written three times; the topmost version is hieroglyphics, the middle version is demotic, and the lower version is Greek. It was discovered in Egypt in 1799 by Napoleon's troops in a town called Rosetta. Later, two men, Thomas Young and Jean Francois Champollion worked together to decipher the hieroglyphics and demotic messages from the Greek, a known language. The work they did served as a "key" that allowed others to decipher hieroglyphics.

According to Gaddis Rose (1987, p. 4) "Human beings need translation for survival: for sharing information daily.… In translation, excellence is comprehensive and vital." Gaddis Rose also writtes "excellence in translation is multidimensional." By excellence she means that the source message is rendered in a manner that is appropriate for the target language audience. In this context, Gaddis Rose uses "appropriate or adequate" to mean suitable for the text in question and suitable for the audience. "Translation is a link between eras, between different civilizations and different peoples" (Lilova, 1987, p. 18).

One early application of written translation was Bible translation. For nearly 2,000 years translators have worked to create accurate translations of the Bible and other holy works, and many books have been written on biblical translation. The demand for accurate translations has spread to many areas of business, commerce, and communication and more books that deal with translation in a broader sense are now available. In the case of biblical or secular translation the emphasis is on preserving the meaning rather than the form of the message. Today many large international companies employ translators to translate documents, instruction manuals, and other written materials. Books, both fiction and non-fiction, are routinely translated from one language to another. More recently, a different use of translation skills has come to the fore. Conferences conducted in American Sign Language or other signed languages may be videotaped and later translated into written English. In such cases the proceedings of the conference can be made available in videotape and in printed form.

Translation is also a link between preinterpreting skills and interpreting skills. Translation requires accurate message preservation across language boundaries. Interpreters who study translation during their preparation can develop a deep understanding of the importance of message equivalence.

Goal of This Book and Video

The purpose of the book and accompanying videotape is to introduce you to the components of translation and guide you toward mastery of translation skills. All of the source materials are in English. Although you may not have had previous opportunity to systematically study translation, this book provides you with specific skills that will build confidence in your translation skills.

In *English Skills Development,* I explain the importance of developing English skills as preparation for translation or interpretation. If English is one of the languages you plan to use as a translator or interpreter, then you must have a high level of proficiency in English. Many authors have written about the importance of language competence in interpreter and translator education, but few emphasize the importance of translation skills in the development of interpretation skills. In translation or interpretation it is important to be sure that the meaning of the original message has been correctly analyzed and understood, as completely as conditions permit.

Translation is not a linear sequence of skills that are performed one at a time. It is a complex series of interacting processes. It can be overwhelming to try to master all the parts of translation at once. Instead, it is more effective to learn how to master the component skills and then learn to synthesize the component skills during the translation process.

Aspects of translation are presented in this workbook. Separating the aspects of translation allows you to experience mastery of the components of the translation process. Systematic development of translation skills that underlie the interpretation process is very important. If these skills are not developed and available, there is a much higher chance that the skills that must follow, such as consecutive interpretation and simultaneous interpretation, will not be strongly grounded. The resulting deficit could lead to interpretations that are skewed or that contain errors. When interpretation skills do not have a firm base, more effort is required during the interpretation process. When more effort is needed, the likelihood of fatigue is increased. Increased fatigue leads to a corresponding increase in errors in interpretation.

This book is designed to provide practice in translation skills that will help ensure that source messages are correctly analyzed and translated. This book is most beneficial if you have completed *Cognitive Processing Skills* and *English Skills Development,* the first two components of *The Effective Interpreting Series.* Strong translation skills are a stepping stone to both professional translation skills and professional simultaneous interpretation skills.

When to Develop Translation Skills

If you are a novice translator, practicing the translation skills in this book provides you with meaningful and well-organized exercises to develop your skills. For the novice interpreter, I suggest that you develop translation skills before moving on to more advanced skills in the interpretation process. If you are beyond the beginning stages of a translator or interpreter education program, or are already a practicing translator or interpreter, you will still benefit from practice in translation skills, either as a refresher or for professional skill maintenance.

How Translators Can Benefit from These Materials

Translators and translators-in-training can benefit from practicing with these materials because the steps of the translation process are divided into categories that correspond to a real translation assignment. The source material was originally spoken and then transcribed. By viewing the accompanying video, translators can get a feel for the effect and intent of the creator of the source text that is ordinarily not available when working from a printed text. Translators and translators-in-training can use the materials in a group educational setting or for individual practice.

The Importance of Translation Skills in Interpreter Education

Developing translation skills can be seen as a discrete step in learning the interpretation process. Even though translation is an important developmental stage in learning interpreting, many interpreter education programs do not directly or fully address the development of translation skills. Taking time to develop translation skills before interpretation skills allows you to work with and realize the importance of developing target language messages that are equivalent to source language messages.

Practicing interpreters may not have had the benefit of studying the individual skills that make up the interpretation process. Developing well-controlled skills in the components of the interpretation process (such as translation skills) can be meaningful and productive practice for the experienced interpreter who wishes to work independently on skill improvement.

The sequence of translation skills presented in this workbook ideally occurs early in a translator or interpreter education program, and can also be used for drills at later stages of development. Each of these skills is relevant to any level of experience in interpretation, beginning, intermediate, or advanced. The source materials themselves can be used again in later stages of training.

Students sometimes experience the "plateau effect" in training. The plateau effect occurs when skills appear to no longer develop as rapidly as they did earlier in the training process. This is a common occurrence. When progress seems to stagnate, it is often useful to go back to an earlier stage of skill development and practice at that level. Taking time to go back and review skills is a positive step because it increases confidence, builds mastery, and often provides the springboard to further progress.

Terminology

The terms you need to know to use the workbook successfully are summarized in alphabetical order below. The intent of the book is to provide you with as much practical experience as possible. To become more familiar with the more theoretical aspects of translation, you may wish to consult the references cited for these terms. In addition, Nida and Tabor (1982) *Theory and Practice of Translation* has an extensive glossary on translations.

Adaptation

Adaptation refers to selection of a culturally equivalent target language response. Bell (1991, p. 71) suggests that in French people say *bon apetit* before eating a meal, but in English the equivalent is silence. Speakers of American English may say nothing or may say something like "dig in" at the beginning of a meal.

Analysis

The analysis stage of translation allows you to consider the meaning of the source text before beginning the transfer process. Nida and Tabor (1982) say that analysis is the stage in which the surface structure is studied to determine the meaning of the words and combinations of the words and grammatical relationships.

Back Translation

Back translation can be used to check the accuracy of a translation. If a text is translated from English to French, the back translation will use the French translation as its starting point, and thus French message will be translated back into English. If the translation from English to French was accurate, then the back translation from French to English will yield an English message that is equivalent to the original English message but may differ in form. Larson (1984) explains that a person who is bilingual in the source and target languages must do the back translation. The back translator should not read the source message and should only translate the target message back into the source language.

Borrowing

Borrowing is a method of choosing lexical equivalents. This means using or borrowing a word directly from the source text and using it in the target text. For example, the word "computer" is used in French, even though it is an English word. The word "computer" will be recognizable in spoken French as the word "computer." This method has application if the source and target language are both spoken or if both languages are signed.

Consecutive Interpreting

According to Gonzalez *et al.* (1991, p. 379), "In consecutive interpreting the interpreter waits until the speaker has finished the source language message before rendering the message into the target language. The duration of the source language may be anywhere from a few seconds to several minutes."

Equivalence

Equivalence is a complex topic and is central to the effectiveness of the translation. Neubert (2000, p. 11) says that equivalence "is the linchpin of translation quality control." Equivalence between the source and target messages depends on the translator's competence in the subject, the culture, and the source and target languages and the ability to convey a concept from the source to the target language adequately. Neubert explains that translation scholars do not agree on a definition of equivalence because equivalence depends on many factors such as the purpose of the translation, the target community, the translator's ability, the context, and the culture.

Form

Nida and Tabor (1982) state that form is the overt or observable structure of discourse such as the words in a language. These authors say that when in a translation, the form of a message must be changed in order to preserve the meaning because languages differ in form. The form conveys the message and is the observable part of the message.

Gloss

"Glosses provide a convenient way to use one language to reference another. Specifically, a gloss is a symbol or group of symbols in one language representing the core meaning of a particular symbol or symbol group from another language. Glosses do not present translations or interpretations and, thus, do not represent natural language use" (Fleetwood, 2001).

Students working between ASL and English will use written English words to *represent* the meanings of ASL signs. A complete glossing system will include non-manual signals as well as information that indicates which sign is meant. In this workbook, you do not need to fill in the non-manual signals unless you are already familiar with such a system. It is very important to realize that there is not a one-to-one correspondence between ASL signs and glosses used to represent the signs.

"When people see an English word used as a gloss, many become confused about the difference between the gloss, the ASL sign that it references, and the English word as it is used in natural interaction. This confusion sometimes leads people who have little familiarity with ASL to think that ASL is a form of English. It is not. The glosses are an invented convention to allow us to make a note about which sign we intend to use in our translation" (Fleetwood, 2001).

Linguists use glosses when they study ASL and need to transcribe the signs they are looking at into a written form. A gloss is usually written in capital letters. For example, the ASL gloss for the English word bike, is BIKE. This does not mean that there is always a one-to-one correspondence between ASL signs and English words. BIKE could also be used as the gloss for the English word bicycle. The English word "run" has many possible glosses in ASL, including DRIP, UNRAVEL, and COMPETE.

It is not necessary to develop a complete and complicated glossing system in order to do the exercises in this workbook. Instead, jot down the gloss for the sign as best you can and then work from your glosses into the signed form of your translation. You will videotape your translation and can refer to the written gloss to help you remember how you want to sign your translation. Try to do so while remembering that a gloss is simply a reference to a core meaning. It is not intended as a natural translation or interpretation.

Idiomatic Translation

Larson (1984) writes that an idiomatic translation uses the natural forms of the target language including grammatical constructions and lexical choices, is natural sounding, and preserves the meaning of the source text. Idiomatic translation is the translator's goal.

Illocutionary Force

The illocutionary force of a message conveys the intent or mood of the speaker. Larson (1984) says that the form of the message reveals the illocutionary force. For example, if the utterance is in the form of a command, it has a different meaning than if it is in the form of a question. The word "Go!" has a different meaning than the word "Go?" The three broad categories of statements, commands or questions include most examples of illocutionary force.

Interpreting

Interpreting is the *process* or activity involved in transferring a message from one language to another in real time, unlike translation, which requires different strategies. The message is usually spoken rather than written. Another feature that distinguishes interpreting from translating is that the interpreter is part of the communication dynamic. Seleskovitch (1978) suggests that the very presence of the interpreter within the communicative event is the major difference between interpretation and translation. According to Gonzalez *et al.*, interpreting is the oral form of the translation process: "Interpreters must instantaneously arrive at a target language equivalent, while at the same time searching for further input" (1991, p. 295).

An Interpretation

Following Bell's (1992) distinctions for a translation, an interpretation is the *product* of the process of interpreting. An interpretation should accurately re-produce the grammatical and lexical features as well as the style and content of the source message.

Literal Translation

According to Larson (1984) a literal translation is one that follows the form of the source language and is nonsensical in the target language. The communication value of a literal translation is low.

Meaning

The meaning is the concept the message expresses. Nida and Tabor (1982) state that each language has its own system of symbolizing meaning. As long as you are dealing within one language this is not an acute problem. When you begin the task of expressing an idea in a language other than the one in which it was originally expressed, many more aspects of meaning come into play. For example, Nida and Tabor point out that each language has a different way of segmenting experience into words (p.21) The general categories for these relationships are listed below.

One-to-Many

This means that one word can have multiple translations, such as the word "run." To translate this word into ASL accurately you must know the context in order to select the most appropriate translation.

Many-to-One

This means that there are many words in the source language but only one in the target language that conveys approximately the same concept

Many-to-Many

This means that many source language words can be related to many target language words, depending on how the words are categorized in the respective languages.

Reformulation

Reformulation is the visible result of the analysis and transfer stages of translation. This is the stage at which the message takes on the *form* of the target language. After you have analyzed and understood the message and transferred it into the target language you will have a product (the translation it-self) or a new form to evaluate, revise, and test.

Risk of Error

Gile (1995, p. 108) says that risk of error can be measured as the likelihood of the translator making the wrong choice or a choice in creating the translation that will skew the meaning.

Simultaneous Interpreting

Gonzalez *et al.* (1991, p. 359) state that simultaneous interpreting is the process wherein the interpreter speaks at the same time as the source language speaker. In this process the source language is rendered into the target language while the source is ongoing. The term "simultaneous interpreting" is really a misnomer because there is always at least a slight delay between the time the original message is spoken and the time the interpretation is delivered.

Source Language

"The source language is the language in which the original author of a message formulated it" (Nida and Tabor, 1982, p. 206). The source language is the language you are translating *from*.

Target Language

"The target language is the language into which the message is being translated" (Gonzalez, *et al.*, 1991, p. 296). This is the language you are translating to. This is sometimes called the receptor language.

Translation Unit

A translation unit is the amount of text that the translator is working with at one time. Ideally the translator works with propositions or concepts, not individual words.

Taxonomy

Taxonomy is a classification system. A taxonomy is a way to organize information. A taxonomy that you will see in this workbook is a system of classifying errors from serious to less serious.

Translation

Bell (1991, p. 13) writes, "Translation is the abstract concept which encompasses both the process of translating and the product of that process."

According to Catford (1965, p. 32) translation involves the substitution of source language meanings with target language meanings. Other authors use the term "transfer" to represent the conveyance of a message from one language to another. It is crucial to realize that the essence of translation deals with meaning preservation across language boundaries, not preservation of form. Nida and Tabor (1982) point out that the writers of a text expect to be understood. Although Nida and Tabor refer primarily to authors of the Bible, the same holds true for other authors. Authors expect to be understood. Translators are obliged to convey the author's message with the same amount of clarity or ambiguity that the original authors used.

Unit of Meaning

Gonzalez *et al.* (1991) suggest that the unit of meaning is the smallest bit of information that cannot be further subdivided but that can be translated. Ordinarily, the word is the smallest unit that can be translated. However, sometimes a phrase is the smallest translatable unit. For example, an idiom is a phrase that must be translated as a meaning unit rather than a series of words. Some examples of idioms are "in the black," which means in a profitable way: "have the last laugh," which means to make someone look foolish, "have it coming," which means to deserve the good or bad things that happen, and "fish or cut bait" which means decide what you want and stop wasting time (Boatner, 1975). These examples show that the meaning of the unit must be correctly understood as idiomatic expressions in order to be translated correctly.

Unduly Free Translation

Larson (1984) explains that an unduly free translation is one that adds information, changes information, leaves out information, or distorts the cultural setting of the source text. The unduly free translation is not the goal of the translator and is generally not acceptable.

These terms will help your understanding when you encounter them in the workbook. Other terms may be introduced within each unit, but these are the basic terms you need to get started on the study of translation. Now that you are familiar with the basic terminology associated with translation, there are other concepts you need to grasp. In addition to terminology you need to know the difference between process and product, what the possible sources of error are in translation, and what specific competencies you need in order to avoid or reduce the risk of making an error in your translation.

Process and Product

In translator and interpreter education there is much discussion over whether students should focus on the process of interpretation or the product of the interpretation. Both are equally important and should be part of even the earliest stages of your training. It is vital that you understand the difference between these two terms and the role they play in your education and training as an interpreter. The process of translation or interpretation is largely invisible. The process is what goes on in your head as you listen, analyze, and transfer the meaning from one language to another. The product, the message rendered in the target language, is the observable result of the process.

The processes associated with the translation or interpretation event cannot be recorded or observed by another person. Only via introspection can interpreters gain insight into their own process and make changes to them. Gile (1995) suggest that adopting a process-oriented approach can optimize training time. In Gile's opinion it is best not to focus solely on the end products of the translation process, but rather to include information on "principles, methods and procedures" (p.10). Gile states, "By concentrating on the reasons for errors or good choices in Translation rather than on the words or structures produced by the students, teachers devote most of their effective teaching time to Translation strategies and lose little time over their by-products" (p.11). Gile further states that later in interpreter training programs, additional emphasis must be placed on the product, but only after the underlying processes are established.

The product is the observable part of your work. It is the message in the target language that the audience receives from the sender via your translation or interpretation. The product can be recorded for future analysis, while the process cannot. Seal (1999, p. 14) has summarized the results of a recent study of sign language interpreters who wished to improve their skills. In that report she emphasizes the importance of analyzing one's own work: "Self-analysis, the zenith of any professional development activity, is highly facilitated when we step back and take a look at ourselves. Routine videotaping and observing videotaped performances for strengths and weaknesses and for changes over time is quite possibly the most valuable, yet least frequently accomplished activity we can engage in." For sign language interpreters, videotaping allows you to review the product. For spoken language interpreters, audiotaping can provide a way to review the product.

It is important to distinguish process from product when developing translation skills. This separation allows you to take time to develop and refine the techniques and thought processes you use to create a product before you become accountable for the product in a professional setting. At the same time the only real way to determine the effectiveness of the processes you use is to evaluate the product itself. Process and product are closely linked and are equally important in translator training.

Sources of Error in Translation

Sources of error in translation are observable by examining the product or finished translation. By focusing on the product alone we can miss important information about the process of translation. By looking at both the process and the product we can obtain a clearer picture of where and why errors occur in translation. Gile (1994) describes a process-oriented approach to training in translation that was developed by the Department of Japanese and Korean Studies of the Institut National des Langues et Civilisations Orientales in Paris. Gile suggests that this process-oriented approach allows for less criticism of the product and greater insight into the process used to create the product. The process-oriented approach allows us to focus on methods used to arrive at translations.

Competencies for Translators and Interpreters

Gonzalez *et al.* (1991, p. 346) and Roberts (1994, p.37) suggest that there are basic competencies that must be in place for interpreters and translators in training as well as for professionals in either field. Although some competencies are shared, the translator does not perform the complex linguistic tasks in real time as the interpreter does. Schaffner and Adab (2000) point out that many scholars and researchers agree that translation consists of "interrelated sub-competencies" and that language competence is necessary but not sufficient. Other important competencies include cultural competence, subject matter competence, and transfer competence. These authors also states that "competence" abilities are based on knowledge.

Linguistic Competence

Roberts (1994) writes that language competence is "the ability to manipulate with ease and accuracy the two languages involved in the interpreting process." This can be subdivided into (1) the ability to understand the source language in all its nuances and (2) the ability to express oneself correctly, fluently, clearly, and with poise in the target language. Neubert (2000, p. 7) writes, "language competence is the *sine qua non* of translation."

Transfer Competence

The next competence that Roberts (1994) addresses is transfer competence. This involves more than understanding the gist of the original message. "Transfer competence includes the ability to understand the articulation of meaning in the source language discourse and the ability to render the meaning of the source language discourse in the target language accurately. Transfer competence also includes the ability to transfer a message from a source language into a target language without undue influence of the source language as well as the ability to transfer a message from a source language into a target language appropriately from the point of view of style."

Neubert (2000) also writes about transfer competence and suggests that transfer comprises the tactics and strategies used to convert texts from the source language to the target language. He says that transfer competence presides over all the other competencies. The other competencies are interrelated and must be combined to achieve translation competence. The actual process of transfer calls into play all of the other competencies and what you know about them.

Methodological Competence

The third important area of competence that Roberts (1994) describes is methodological competence. Roberts says that there are two subcategories within methodological competence. The first is knowing which mode (consecutive or simultaneous) to use for a given setting. The other subcategory is the ability to find pertinent lexical and terminological data, or appropriate vocabulary, and to use it correctly.

Bicultural Competence

The fourth area of competence that Roberts explores is bicultural competence. By this she means "deep knowledge and appreciation of the cultures underlying the working languages, is based on the concept that language is a reflection of culture and that true understanding of a message involves not only a mastery of the language in which it is expressed but of the culture the language represents. Bicultural competence includes knowledge of the basic beliefs, values, experiences and behaviors characteristic of source language speakers and target language speakers." Appreciation of the differences between source and target language cultures is also included in bicultural competence.

Discourse Competence

There are other competencies that are important for translators and interpreters. According to Widdowson (1978), discourse competence is important. This competence is defined as "the ability to combine ideas into a coherent, cohesive set," and includes the ability to formulate a complete idea using appropriate pronouns and connectors appropriately.

Sociolinguistic Competence

Gonzalez *et al.* (1991) emphasize the importance of sociolinguistic competence or the ability to appropriately use register, or levels of formality or informality. Sociolinguistic competence includes the ability to use the appropriate speech style for a given setting, such as court or an informal meeting.

Creativity

Neubert (2000) discusses additional aspects of translation competencies and points out that because translators are not necessarily experts in the subjects that they translate, they must acquire the capacity to *approximate* the subject areas to an extent that allows understanding. Neubert suggests that this competence must be open-ended. "Translators are always on the lookout for new ways of saying something. They must always feel the pulse of language" (p.4). The need to be open-ended or flexible leads to the need for *creativity* because the source text and the context in which it occurred must be expressed in a different language, with different linguistic and cultural constraints. Creativity in this sense does not mean rendering a translation that has little or no relationship to the source text. Instead it means that the translator must be flexible enough to render a translation that preserves the meaning in either a general or specific manner, depending on the translator's skill and background knowledge of the subject.

Kussmaul (1995) stresses the need for creativity in translation. He describes a model of the creative process that includes four phases: preparation, incubation, illumination, and evaluation. As observed by Kussmaul, these phases were first proposed by Poincare (1913; cf Landau, 1969). The phases do not necessarily occur in a linear fashion, but can occur simultaneously. We cannot observe any of the stages and cannot say that they occur in isolation or even that they occur one after the other.

In the preparation phase detection and analysis of problems occur and knowledge is accumulated. Kussmaul (1995) states this stage corresponds to comprehension of the source text, when the function of the text is established. Noticing problems and finding relevant information to help solve the problem is a part of the creative process.

The incubation stage is linked with the ability to find many thoughts and ideas related to solving a problem in a short period of time (Guilford, 1975). In order to encourage productivity during incubation, Kussmaul suggests the technique of *brainstorming*. Once the problem is identified, members of a translation team are encouraged to come up with all kinds of suggestions and possible solutions without evaluating them. During this phase it is important to relax and let the ideas flow. Sometimes you need to simply "let your mind alone," and during this time relevant ideas and solutions may surface. Existing information can be reorganized when you take a break from the translation brainstorming process for a few minutes. "At a conscious level the mind is at rest, but at the same time, mental activity goes on subconsciously" (Kussmaul, 1995, p. 44).

The last two stages, illumination and *evaluation* are very closely linked. It is difficult to separate the feeling of "Aha, I have found a translation that works" from "yes, this translation is accurate!" Alternatively, you might think that you have found an adequate translation and then suddenly realize that it is not adequate. Using creativity in translation does not mean that you invent or make up solutions to translation problems. Instead it means using your linguistic resources to come up with a faithful translation.

Translators and interpreters need a variety of linguistic and non-linguistic competencies in order to create faithful translations. Creativity is an important part of the translation process and may have been overlooked. As you do the exercises in the units that follow think about the four stages of the creative process and apply them to your translations. Next we will consider models of translation. Having a mental framework for the translation process can help organize the stages of translation and can be an effective way to think about the complex process of translation.

Models of Translation

There are many models of translation. Each model attempts to describe the stages in the translation process. It is difficult to describe the translation process because much of the translation process cannot be directly observed.

Models show us that there are many decisions to be made during the translation process. Some models have many boxes, squares, and arrows to represent the possible stages in the translation process and the relationships between the stages. Other models are more general in approach and describe the main stages in the process. In looking at either a detailed or a global model, it is important to remember that each model represents a theoretical opinion about what happens in the translation process. Models are useful when one is studying translation because the models help break down a complex process into smaller pieces that can be studied and mastered. It is important to be able to manage the parts of the process before attempting to synthesize, or combine, the parts in the translation process. As we compare three models of translation we look for similarities between models that can help us.

Three models are described below. Translation models are not rules for translation; they simply show how the theorist who devised the model sees the interrelationship of the stages of the process. Nida and Tabor use the term restructuring while Gile uses the term reformulation to describe roughly the same parts of the translation process. In this book we use the term reformulation.

Nida and Tabor's Model

Nida and Tabor (1982) present a three-stage model of translation that includes (1) analysis, (2) transfer, and (3) restructuring. They write that the analysis stage is the stage in which "the message is analyzed in terms of the grammatical relationships and the meanings of the words and combinations of the words." They describe the transfer stage as the stage in "which the analyzed material is transferred in the mind of the translator from language A to language B." The transfer stage cannot be directly observed. The third stage is restructuring, which means that the message is rendered in a form that is acceptable in the target language.

Gile's Sequential Model of Translation

Gile (1995) describes a two-stage model of translation. The two stages are comprehension and reformulation. Gile states that this model represents an "idealized process" that can help beginning translators focus on the important stages in the translation process. He writes that the model is a "guiding tool for translation methodology during initial training" (p. 107). He goes on to state that it is important to begin with texts that can be easily comprehended so that you can become comfortable using the two-stage model. In Gile's model the reformulation phase includes stages that Nida and Tabor call transfer and reformulating.

Gile cautions that translation is not really a linear process with well-defined boundaries between stages that always progress from comprehension to reformulation. Instead, the process may be more like a back-and-forth movement between the two stages. For example, in the comprehension phase you establish what Gile calls a *meaning hypothesis,* in which you temporarily assign a meaning to the part of the text you are working on. This temporary meaning is based on what you already know about the topic, what you can logically infer, and what you can find out. Next you check the meaning hypothesis for plausibility. Does the meaning hypothesis make sense in this context? Gile says that errors can occur if you read the text too fast or do not have the background knowledge to fully understand the text. Once you are satisfied that the meaning hypothesis is plausible, you can go on to the reformulation phase.

According to Gile, in the reformulation phase, you verbalize the meaning of the text in the target language and then check to be sure that all the relevant information is included and that extraneous information is not included. Sometimes you will need to create more than one version. You must also check the target language version of the text for correct terminology and style. If you find some areas in the text that are not acceptable, then you continue the process until the results are grammatically acceptable and plausible.

Bell's Model of Translation

Bell (1991) suggests a model that accounts for the fact that translation is not a linear event with strict stages that must occur in a specified order. "It is an integrated process in which, although every stage must be passed through, the order is not fixed and back tracking, revision and cancellation of previous decisions are the norm rather than the exception" (p. 45). Bell's model includes a detailed description for each stage of the translation process. Bell summarizes his model into three salient phases: "(1) Analysis of the source language text, (2) organization of the semantic representations of the individual clauses into an integrated schema and, (3) synthesis of the new target language text" (p. 61).

In comparing the three models outlined here, Nida and Tabor's, Giles, and Bell's, we find similarities. We see that even though each model labels the stages differently, the models share as a starting point the importance of fully understanding and analyzing the message before beginning the translation process. They all agree that the translation must be faithful to the original text and that the translation process involves reworking the translation more than once. They agree that the central portion of the process, transfer, is invisible. They share a common goal of finding a way to make the translation process and its discrete, yet interrelated, phases understandable and accessible to students and translators alike.

This unit introduces you to three models of translation, each having its own terminology and emphasis. While studying translation it is helpful to find a simple and clear way to think about a complex process as you learn how to render faithful translations. This workbook uses a three-stage model that combines the aspects of the models described above. The three stages are 1.) analysis, 2.) transfer, and 3.) reformulation. Each of these stages is addressed in the units that follow. Although we focus on one stage at a time, remember that the stages really do not occur in isolation except for purposes of study.

Study Questions

1. Write a short well-organized essay explaining the differences and similarities between translation and interpretation. Be sure your essay has an introduction and conclusion.

_____

_____

_____

_____

_____

_____

_____

_____

_____

_____

_____

_____

_____

_____

_____

_____

_____

_____

_____

_____

_____

_____

_____

_____

_____

_____

2. Write a short well-organized essay explaining the differences between source language and target language. Be sure your essay has an introduction and conclusion.

_____

_____

_____

_____

_____

_____

_____

_____

_____

_____

_____

3. Write a short well-organized essay explaining the differences between form and meaning. Be sure your essay has an introduction and conclusion.

_____

_____

_____

_____

_____

_____

_____

_____

_____

_____

_____

_____

_____

_____

4. Write a well-organized essay describing what the meaning of the terms "one-to-many" and "many-to-one." Give examples. Be sure your essay has an introduction and conclusion.

_____

_____

_____

_____

_____

_____

_____

_____

_____

_____

_____

_____

_____

_____

_____

_____

_____

_____

_____

5. Describe Nida and Tabor's model of translation. Present your answer in a well-organized essay.

_____

_____

_____

_____

_____

_____

_____

_____

_____

_____

_____

_____

_____

_____

UNIT

1

Preparing to Translate

Introduction

This unit introduces factors you must consider during the preparation phase of a translation project and suggests some basic approaches to the translation project. Taking time to prepare a translation project allows you to estimate how much time you need to complete the project and to decide if the project is within your current skill range. The factors to consider are the purpose of the translation, length of the text and time frame for completion function of the text, expected audience, your competence in the source and target languages, and your competence in the subject area. This unit also includes a series of methods to use when translating.

Nida and Tabor (1982) say that a translation should reproduce the message from one language into another while keeping the meaning as constant as possible and secondly keeping the style of the original as much as possible when the message is rendered into the target language. These authors say that the best translation does not seem like a translation; the translation should seem natural while preserving the message and intent of the speaker. In order to achieve a natural translation that preserves as much of the meaning as possible, it is necessary to master each of the skills that make up the translation process. In order to know which skills you need, you must first consider the factors related to the translation process.

Factors in Translation

There are a variety of factors that play a role in creating a translation. Some of the many factors are summarized here to give you an overview of the things you should consider before and during the translation process.

Purpose

The translator needs to know the purpose of the translation. Will the translation be used as a brochure, a legal text, a published document, a literary manuscript, or some other form? Fraser (2000) suggests that the purpose of the translation along with a description of the expected readership provide a basis for many decisions to be made by the translator during the translation process. Fraser says that translators need this information, but often do not get it from their clients. If you do not know the purpose of the translation, you should consider asking the client for this information. Nord (1995) says that if you know the purpose of the translation and the intended readership, you are likely to make fewer mistakes in translation. Vermeer (1989) agrees that knowing the purpose of the translation can improve the accountability of the translation. Finally, Fraser (2000) reminds us that if the information we need to have before we can proceed with a translation is not provided, we may need to be assertive in requesting relevant information. Once you have determined the purpose of the text you can move on to the function of the text.

Function of the Text

The function of the text is the author's or speaker's intent. The function comprises the context in which the utterances occur and the actual words the speaker uses. The example that Kussmaul (1995) gives is the use of the word "bloody" in the context of a British school child calling a teacher "a bloody fool." To fully understand the usage of the word, you must understand the context in which it occurred and the speaker's intent. The word "bloody" in this context has nothing to do with blood, but is used as an adjective to modify the word "fool." There are nonlinguistic aspects of the function of the text, such as the facial expressions, tone of voice, manner of signing, body language, and gestures. All of these nonlinguistic or paralinguistic features contribute to the meaning of the individual words. Knowing the function of the text allows you to better convey the speaker's intent.

Expected Audience

You must prepare your translation for an audience, just as the original author did. "No translation should be undertaken without a clear understanding of who will use it." (Larson, 1984 p. 468). Sometimes the author or publisher will describe the intended audience. Alternatively you may not know for whom the original text was intended but you must use deductive reasoning skills to determine the audience for the translation. For example, as you read the source text, Larson suggests that you must infer the nature of the original audience. Was it intended for children, or adults, or specialists in a particular field? What are the respective levels of education of the source and target audience? Then imagine a roughly equivalent group of people who do not speak the source language. The translation must be true to the intent, message, and tone of the source text and have the same effect on the target language audience as the source message did on the original audience (Larson 1987). Knowing your audience or seeking out as much information as you can about the expected audience will make the translation more relevant and meaningful.

Length and Time Frame

The overall length of the project sometimes determines the rate of pay for the translator. It is important to have a feel for the overall length of the project to establish an appropriate pay scale and time frame for completing the translation. The length of the source text, the translator's skill, and the due date will affect the time frame for completion of the translation. To plan your workload appropriately, you will need to make a reasonable projection regarding the amount of time needed to complete the translation. Sometimes your available time and the timeframe of the translation do not match. When you can determine this in advance of accepting the assignment, you can save you and your client disappointment.

Competencies Related to the Translation Process

There are at least three main areas of competence that are important for translators and interpreters.

Competence in the Target Language

The target language is the language you are translating into. If you are translating into your first language, and if you have a good command of your first language, the translation should be natural sounding and should contain all of the information and impact of the original message. If the target language is your second language the translation may sound less natural than if you are working into your first language. The ideal but rare situation is when your linguistic skills in both the source and the target language are equally strong. It is more common to have stronger skills in your first language than in your second.

Competence in the Source Language

If the source language is your first language, comprehension of the source language is generally easier than if the source language is your second language. Do not assume, though, that native speakers of English or any other language do not need to study in order to improve their skills. Translators and interpreters who study their first language have fewer difficulties understanding the intent and message of the source text. If the source text is in your second language you may experience more difficulties in understanding the message.

Competence with the Subject Area

During the preparation phase you must also consider the subject matter. Is this a subject about which you are knowledgeable? Do you know how to find the background information you need? You must answer these questions objectively and then decide if you can proceed with the project. If it is an area that is outside of your competence, then you must decide if you can get sufficient background information through research. If you depend on research to fill in your subject area competence, you must also realize that there will be a greater risk of lost information if you are not truly conversant with the topic.

When considering the subject matter, it is important to recognize that if you have strong philosophical or ethical positions that conflict with those of the subject matter, you may not be able to render an objective translation. Strong feelings about a topic might prevent you from being able to translate effectively and faithfully.

After you have considered the factors in the translation project, and the competency areas of source language, target language and subject matter, you are ready to begin the steps in the translation process.

Steps in the Translation Process

So far we have looked at some of the basic questions to consider when preparing to translate. Once you have a general idea of what the translation project will involve and have decided that your level of competence matches the needs of the project, then you can consider which translation methods to use. This overview of methodology allows you to begin your translations in this unit. As you progress through the workbook additional translation methods are emphasized.

Various authors, including Nida and Tabor and Larson, have described the steps in translation. The following is a summary of the methods suggested by Nida, Tabor, and Larson. Some of these methods are described in more detail in other units of this workbook. This summary provides an overview of the considerations in the translation process.

Analyze the Source Text

A summary of analysis follows. Unit 2 deals with analysis in more depth.

Find the Main Idea of the Entire Text

After considering some of the more global aspects of the translation project as mentioned above, you must first find the gist or main idea of the text. To do this you must read over the entire text and then select the ideas that are most central and the ideas that are less central.

Find the Main Idea of Each Paragraph

After finding the main idea or gist of the source text, the next step is to find the main idea of each paragraph and begin making an outline of the main ideas contained in the source text. It is best to create the outline in the target language. If the target language is a signed language, then you can video-record main ideas in the target language. You can also use glossing as an intermediate step if you are working into a signed language.

Identify Specific Translation Issues

In examining the text you are sure to find ideas or words whose meaning is not entirely clear to you. Write these down and then work to find out the meaning of these special areas. Keep another list for terms and ideas that you understand but do not know how to express in the target language.

Thus you will have two lists of special issues: one list containing words or ideas whose meaning is unclear and a second containing words and ideas that you do understand but do not know how to express in the target language. Take the first list and reconsider each term in its context. Sometimes knowing how a word is used in a sentence will reveal its meaning. If not, select several possible meanings that the term could have in this context. Try out several options and see which makes the best sense in the context and keeps the intent of the speaker in mind. You can also check with native speakers of the source text to gain insight into how these terms could be used. Consulting a dictionary or thesaurus helps you understand terms in the source text. Dictionaries for signed languages are scarce, and if they exist, they may show signs in two dimensions. Signs are really three-dimensional. Moreover, sign language dictionaries often show signs in isolation rather than in context and so are of limited value. Checking with an experienced user of the signed language may be the best resource.

Once you have addressed all the issues on the first list, you can begin to address the issues on the second list. Look for expressions in the target language that accurately convey the source message. For example, idiomatic expressions in the source language require expressions in the target language that convey the same idea. A word-for-word or literal translation will undoubtedly lose the meaning of the original. You can record your attempts at rendering the message in the target language and ask a native speaker if the resulting translation is natural. You can also work with a study group or your teacher to find appropriate target language expressions.

Transfer

Transfer is summarized here and discussed in more depth in Unit 3. Larson (1984, p.480) states "Transfer is the process of going from the semantic structure analysis to the initial draft of the translation. Transfer takes place in the mind of the translator." Transfer is the process that results in the observable product of a translation in the target language. Nida and Tabor (1982, p.99) write, "…transfer itself is the crucial and focal point of the translation process."

Reformulation

After analyzing and transferring the message, you express or reformulate it in the target language. The visible result of reformulation is the draft translation and, later the finished translation. Reformulation is discussed in more depth in Unit 4.

Create a Draft

The next step in translation is creating a draft of the entire text. It is best to have the entire text in mind as you work through the parts of the translation. The first draft allows you to note areas that you want to improve and gives you an idea of how much more work is needed to complete the translation.

Review and Revise

After you have completed the draft and revised the translation, read the entire source text and then read the translation. See if the overall gist is preserved in the translation. If order of events is crucial to the message, check that the main ideas are preserved and presented in the same order. Check that the meaning of idiomatic expressions in the source language has been adequately conveyed in the target language. If particular areas need work, revise the translation to the best of your ability. The amount that you revise will depend on your skill and the amount of time that you have to complete the translation.

Translate the Title

Translating the title after the main text ensures that you have a better idea of what is contained in the body of the text. Knowing the content of the text, the intent of the original author, and the intended audience allows you to more accurately translate the title.

Test the Translation

Gile (1995) says that the translator must test the translation for editorial acceptability, clarity, language correctness, stylistic appropriateness, and terminological usage. He says the translation must be faithful to the original message and acceptable in the target language. Other aspects of testing the translation include evaluating the impact of the text before and after translation, having the translation peer reviewed, and back translation.

Impact of the Source Text

The impact of the source text must be preserved in the target text. The intent of any communication is called illocutionary force. The translation should have the same impact on its readers as the source text did on its readers. You may not be able to find out the impact on the original audience, but you can note the impact of the source text on you and try to replicate an equivalent impact in the target language text.

Peer Review

After you have completed the steps outlined above, ask a fellow translator to review the source text and translation to check for accuracy. The peer review process requires additional time beyond the time needed for the translation itself. Even though peer review is an excellent way to check a translation, due to time or other constraints, it is not always possible to have your translation reviewed by another translator.

Back Translation

Sometimes back translation is used to check the accuracy of a translation. The translation is translated back into the source language and then compared with the original source language text. The back translation and the original text should be equivalent in meaning. It is unlikely that the source text and back translation will be exactly the same even though both present the message in the same language. A bilingual individual who has not examined the source message should do the back translation.

Consider Risk of Error and Loss

Sometimes there are unforeseen problems that negatively affect your translation. Gile (1985) points out that his model of translation does not account for what happens when translation problems cannot be resolved. If you do not have access to the information you need, adequate time, or linguistic or financial resources to solve a problem, then you must do the best translation you can. The realization that you do not have all the resources you need may become apparent only after you have accepted the translation assignment. If you are faced with the obligation to complete the project, but do not have access to all the information you need, then the issue Gile calls *risk of error and loss* must be considered.

Gile (1995, p. 108) says that risk of error indicates the likelihood of the translator making the wrong choice. It is important to keep in mind that linguistic issues are seldom black or white. "Wrong" in this case means that the decision process that the translator used led to a skew in the message and possibly its impact. Wrong choices can include choosing the wrong technical term, erroneously interpreting an ambiguous statement, or other faulty decisions. "Loss refers to the potential consequences of such an error. Possible consequences include those that will affect the author, the readers, and the client: loss of information, wrong information, loss of impact with respect to the author's aims" (p. 108). Gile suggests that when risk of error and loss cannot be avoided, you should try for the best combination of risk and loss for the situation. For example, if you cannot find the exact term that you need in the target language, that is an error, but if you can accurately describe the concept in a series of terms then there may not be any significant loss of message. Conversely, if you choose a single term that conveys the wrong message, the risk of error is great and so is the loss.

Preparing for Translation vs. Interpretation

There are some important similarities and differences between translation and interpretation with regard to the preparation process. Interpreters work in real time and cannot read and review the source message before and after interpreting it. Nevertheless, some of the steps that translators use are the same steps that interpreters use. The following is a comparison between the two processes.

Translators and interpreters both need to have specialized training and preparation in advance of beginning their professional work. Assuming that proper and sufficient training is in place, preparation for a specific translation or interpretation can be undertaken. With regard to length, the translator can see the entire text as a whole, before beginning the translation, while the interpreter may only know the number of hours the assignment is expected to last but may not have access to the content in advance. In both translation and interpretation, competence in the source and target languages as well as in the subject matter is of great importance.

The time frame for the translation will depend on variables such as availability of reference materials, speed at which the translator can work, and availability of peer reviewers who can work in a timely fashion. For the interpreter the time frame is set by the length of time that the speaker talks (or signs) or is scheduled to talk. With regard to the audience, the translator usually has no direct contact with either the original audience or the audience that the translation reaches. In contrast, the interpreter has direct and immediate interaction with the audience while interpreting. Direct contact with the audience allows the interpreter to have feedback about the impact of the text on the audience, while the translator must use inference to deduce the impact of the message on the audience.

Other comparisons between translation and interpretation include methodological factors. The translator can find the main idea while reading through the text before translating it while the interpreter must figure out the main idea in real time while listening to an ongoing spoken or signed message. The translator can isolate translation problems and solve them, but the interpreter must make quick decisions about what is not clear and ask for clarification or repetition. The issue of risk of error and loss is present for both the translator and the interpreter. Both the translator and the interpreter may have a better chance of reducing the amount of loss if they are aware of ambiguities and other aspects of the source language that are difficult to translate. Awareness of ambiguity leads to the effort to clarify, which can reduce loss.

The translator can create a draft while the interpreter cannot. The interpreter must commit to their rendition of the message into the target language in real time. The translator can review and revise, while the interpreter cannot. The interpreter's work is evanescent, which means that it vanishes and cannot be reinspected or changed once it is rendered. The translator translates the title after reflection and developing insight into the meaning and intent of the text while the interpreter renders the title, if any, in real time. The translator can use peer review while the interpreter does not have access to this exact kind of input. Instead, the interpreter may have a partner who monitors and provides correction and support in real time and may even provide feedback after the fact. After-the-fact feedback from another interpreter may help improve future performances but cannot improve the performance already rendered.

Some of the similarities and differences in the preparation phase and methodological approaches for the translator and interpreter should now be apparent. The differences are governed by the fact that the interpreter must work in real time while the translator does not. The translator's process includes an overview of the project, review and revision, consultation with peers, and additional revision if necessary. While the focus of these materials is translation, for those becoming interpreters, it is good to be aware of these differences.

The Role of Intuition in Translation

This section discusses the importance of developing intuition about the translation process that supercedes a rule-governed approach to translation. Once you have mastered the skills within translation in a predictable and discrete manner, it is important to value the role of intuition. Chesterman (2000) states "Intuition is the driving force of skilled behavior, an intuition that is trusted because it is constantly tested and refined." It is important to develop a trust in your own work that is grounded in technique and experience. After you become an expert you may not even recall or be aware of the stages that you went through as you developed the skill. Instead you may just have a feeling that the translation "feels just right."

Translation expertise usually develops in predictable stages. According to Dreyfus and Dreyfus (1986) there are five stages of expertise. The first is the *novice* stage, in which the student must learn the facts, features, and rules related to the skill, as defined by the teacher. This stage requires fully conscious decision making. The next stage is *advanced beginner*, in which you begin to generalize some of the rules and facts and can see how the context affects the rules and facts. The third stage is the *competence* stage, in which the features of the situation become more relevant and must be prioritized. The competence stage is when decision making becomes more important because you can now grasp the larger picture and the translation task as a whole. The competence stage is distinct from the first two stages because it requires personal responsibility for decision making. The first two stages did not because they were simply rule-governed behaviors.

The fourth stage is *proficiency*, where *intuition* and experience play larger roles. "Intuition and rationality are used alternately, so that the trainee is sometimes inside what the Dreyfuses call the 'world of the skill'" (Dreyfus & Dreyfus 1986, p.29). In the proficiency stage the separate parts of the process no longer seem separate and performing the skill seems more fluid. In this stage the translator may even feel detached from the translation process. The fifth and final stage is *expertise*. Intuition dominates this stage. Expertise is the combination of intuition and carefully developed skills that are constantly tested. "Between the moments of monitoring, expert performance is experienced as a feeling of flow, euphoria in which the performer is lost in the performance, totally involved in the task even though the monitoring mind remains on guard" (Chesterman, 2000, p.79).

Chesterman explains that the growth of expertise is a gradual one and that emotional involvement and intuition play important roles in expertise. He states that the detached and analytical thinking gradually gives way to intuition. Intuition gradually provides internal feedback that guides the expert. The Dryfuses sum it up this way "Skill in any domain is measured by the performer's ability to act appropriately in situations that might once have been problems but are no longer problems and so do not require analytic reflection" (Dreyfus and Dreyfus 1986, p.156). This means that the more you practice and refine your skills in translation, the more intuition you will have about your translation processes.

Preparation Exercises

With this basic background information and an outline of the steps used to create a translation, you are ready to do the exercises in this unit.

EXERCISE 1.1

Introduction
CHRIS LEWNES

Directions

Find and listen to this selection on your videotape. Write a description of the intended audience in the space following. Stop the tape and read the transcript of this passage. Before attempting a translation, answer the first four study questions related to this passage. The fifth study question asks you to translate the passage while keeping track of how long you take to do so. If you are working into a signed language, you may write the translation in gloss form and then work from the glosses and videotape yourself signing the translation of the passage. If you are working into a written language write your translation in the space below the passage. Then do the follow-up.

_____

_____

Transcript for *Introduction,* by Chris Lewnes

1   Hello. My name is Chris Lewnes. I'm a retired Navy pilot originally

2   from New Jersey. The Navy brought me here to San Diego, which is a

3   beautiful place to be. I've since settled here in the Scripps Ranch area

4   with my wife and two daughters.

_____

_____

_____

_____

_____

_____

Study Questions

1. What is the purpose of this translation? One aspect of the preparation phase is creating an estimate of how long it will take you to complete the translation. How much time do you estimate you will need to translate this passage? What is the function of the text?

_____

_____

_____

2. Describe your level of competence in the source and target languages. What is your level of competence with regard to the subject matter? With regard to methodological competence which words will you need to look up? Do you need to solve any special linguistic problems?

_____

_____

_____

3. Find the main idea of the text and write it in one sentence.

_____

_____

_____

4. What is the risk of error in this passage? What does this risk depend on? What is the risk of loss? What does this risk depend on?

_____

_____

_____

_____

5. Refer back to the list of considerations in this unit and write down an estimated time to complete a translation of this passage. Now complete your translation, keeping track of how long it takes you. Write down the difference between the estimated time and the actual time that it took to translate the passage.

_____

_____

_____

_____

Sample Five-Step Follow-up—Pat's Answers

Since this is the first time you have encountered the follow-up, the progress of a hypothetical student named Pat is discussed here to help you get started on your own five-step follow-up. Write your answers in this book or record them on videotape.

Here are Pat's answers to each part of the five-step follow-up for Exercise 1.1.

Step 1   Observation

Review your answers.

Pat watched the selection, answered the study questions, and rendered the translation of the selection. Since all three parts are completed, Pat makes a note that all three parts are finished and goes on to the second step in the follow-up.

Step 2   Selection

Underline or otherwise note the portions of your translation that are most satisfactory. Circle any portions that need further attention.

Pat has no prior experience with translation or in preparing to translate. Pat finds that the translation process was more time consuming than expected for such a short passage. Pat thought it would take about 5 minutes to do the preparation phase and the translation. It really took 15 minutes for the preparation phase and 15 minutes to translate.

Pat did not realize that the words "originally" and "settled" would be difficult to translate. After working on the translation Pat realized that these two words are special problems at this stage of development and need extra attention in translation. For step 2 of the follow-up, Pat notes that further attention is needed in identifying special translation problems and in estimating how much time the translation will require. Pat can use the counter on the VCR to note which parts of the ASL translation need improvement.

Step 3   Analysis

Analyze for accuracy.

Error analysis is one way to reveal what is happening during the translation process. It is usually easier to analyze errors than analyze places where the translation was correct. Error analysis is standard practice in translation and interpretation teaching and testing. In the analysis step of the follow-up Pat has to remember that in this unit the emphasis is on the preparation phase of translation. During the preparation phase Pat knew that s/he accurately understood the passage, had enough language competence to translate it into the source language, had sufficient subject area competence, could find the main idea, and realized that there was not much risk of error. Pat needs to continue to work on identifying special translation problems and accurately estimating how much time is required to render the translation.

Step 4   Assessment

Assessment allows you to determine the *effect* of any errors on the overall translation.

In English Skills Development *and* Cognitive Processing in English, *the emphasis was on finding the reasons for the errors. According to Kussmaul (2000) finding reasons for errors is appropriate for language teaching, but in the case of translation, it is more relevant to determine the communicative function of the error. For example, does the error distort the message or is there a "sufficient degree of precision?" In Kussmaul's communicative approach to translation evaluation, the focus is on the effect of the translation on the target reader, not on what the translator was thinking while creating the translation. Kussmaul's approach focuses on the product.*

For example, omitting the preparation phase could lead to errors in the translation if you accept a translation assignment that you are not prepared for or qualified to complete. Consider your understanding of the preparation phase as it relates to translation. In this step, Pat looks at how well s/he understands the importance of the preparation phase in translation and how well s/he performs the preparation and notes any areas that are unclear or confusing about the preparation phase.

Step 5   Action

Develop a plan for action based on your analysis and assessment.

In the fifth step Pat reviews the work in steps 1 through 4 and writes a plan of action to improve performance. For example, Pat decides to allow more time when estimating how much time the translation will require. The estimates will be more accurate when Pat is better able to identify special translation problems. The translation problems of finding good expressions to convey "originally" and "settled" in the target language took longer than expected. Pat wanted to know where Scripps Ranch is located and looked on the World Wide Web to find it. In future exercises, Pat will look carefully for translation problems and that will help provide a more accurate estimate of how much time the translation will require.

Remember that allowing time for research is a necessary component of translation. You need to be as well informed as you can about the topic. You often will not have had the time to research the specific topic and you also may not have the necessary background information. These two common facts can weaken an interpretation but are an everyday reality for most interpreters.

As a result of the follow-up, Pat realizes that the preparation phase is an important part of the translation process because it helps to determine how much time, effort, and skill the translation will require.

Five-Step Follow-up

Complete the preparation phase, answers to the study questions, and your translation before you do the follow-up.

Step 1   Observation

Review your responses.

Step 2   Selection

Underline or otherwise identify the portions of your translation that are most satisfactory and circle any portions of the source text that you were unable to translate. With regard to the circled portions, could you translate those sections with additional preparation?

Step 3   Analysis

Analyze your work in the preparation phase and then the translation. Was your preparation complete? One way to analyze your translation for accuracy is by comparing the message conveyed by the source language with the message conveyed by the target language. List the propositions in the source and target language in the space provided and compare them for meaning.

_____

_____

_____

_____

Step 4   Assessment

Assess the preparation phase and then the translation itself. What was the effect of the preparation phase on the translation?

_____

_____

_____

_____

Step 5   Action

Develop a plan for action based on your analysis and assessment.

In the action step you review what you have discovered about your work in steps 1 through 4 and make some decisions about what action you will take to take to improve your performance in the preparation phase of translation. A suggested activity is to select another passage and prepare to translate it. Then translate it and see if your estimate of the time required is more accurate. Write your action plan below.

_____

_____

_____

_____

EXERCISE 1.2

Bike with Flat Tire
DIANA GORMAN

Directions

Find and listen to this selection on your videotape. Write a description of the intended audience in the space provided. Stop the tape and read the transcript of "Bike with Flat Tire." Answer the first four study questions. For the fifth study question translate the passage into the target language, keeping track of how long this takes you. If you are working into a signed language, write the translation in gloss form and then work from the glosses to a videotaped version of this passage. If you are working into a written language write your translation in the space provided below the passage. Do the follow-up.

_____

_____

Transcript for *Bike with Flat Tire,* by Diana Gorman

1   The girl is walking her bike, which has a flat tire. She then fills it up

2   with air. She then happily rides off.

_____

_____

_____

_____

Study Questions

1. What is the purpose of this translation? How much time do you estimate you will need to translate this passage? What is the function of the text?

_____

_____

_____

_____

2. Describe your level of competence in the source and target languages. What is your level of competence with regard to the subject matter? With regard to methodological competence which words will you need to look up? Do you need to solve any special linguistic problems?

_____

_____

3. Find the main idea and write it in one sentence in English.

_____

_____

_____

_____

4. What is the risk of error in this passage? What does this risk depend on? What is the risk of loss? What does this risk depend on?

_____

_____

_____

_____

5. Refer back to the list of considerations in this unit and write down an estimate of the time that you need to translate the passage. Now complete your translation, keeping track of how long it takes you. Write down the difference between the estimated time and the actual time that it took to translate the passage.

_____

_____

_____

_____

Five-Step Follow-up

Your translation and answers to all the study questions should be completed before you do the follow-up process.

Step 1   Observation

This step allows you to observe your work objectively. Review your responses.

Step 2   Selection

Underline or otherwise indicate the portions of your translation that are most satisfactory and circle any portions of the source text that you were unable to translate. With regard to the circled portions, could you translate those sections with additional preparation?

Step 3   Analysis

Analyze your work in the preparation phase and then the translation. Was your preparation complete? One way to analyze your translation for accuracy is by comparing the message conveyed by the source language with the messagae conveyed by the target language. List the propositions in the source and target language in the space provided and compare them for meaning.

_____

_____

_____

_____

Step 4   Assessment

The assessment in this case is of the preparation phase and then the translation itself. What was the effect of preparation on the translation?

_____

_____

_____

_____

Step 5   Action

Develop a plan for action based on your analysis and assessment.

In the fifth step you review what you have discovered about your work in steps 1 through 4 and write the steps you will take to improve your performance. A suggested activity is to consider the role of classifiers in the translation. If your command of the use of classifiers or other special aspects of language such as verb conjugations is weak, you know you must allow more time for the translation. Write your action plan in the space below.

_____

_____

_____

_____

EXERCISE 1.3

Directions to My Office
RICHARD SOMERVILLE

Directions

Find and listen to this selection on your videotape. Write a description of the intended audience in the space provided. Stop the tape and read the transcript of this passage. Then answer the first four study questions related to this passage. The fifth study question asks you to translate the passage into the target language, keeping track of how long this takes you. If you are working into a signed language, you may write the translation in gloss form and then videotape a signed version of this passage. If you are working into a written language write your translation in the space provided after the passage. Do the follow-up.

_____

_____

Transcript for *Directions to My Office*, by Richard Somerville.

1   My name is Richard Somerville. I'm going to give you directions to
2   my office from the San Diego airport. When you land at the airport
3   and rent a car, ask for directions to Interstate 5, everybody knows
4   how to get to I 5, and get on I 5 going north.

5   After about 15 minutes look for the exit La Jolla Village Drive and
6   take that exit. When you get off the freeway, turn left. You'll be going
7   west towards the ocean; you'll cross back over the freeway. And then
8   keep on going on La Jolla Village Drive until you see the campus on
9   your right. You'll go up a hill, and when it finally levels out look for a
10 sign to the left for the Steven Birch Aquarium Museum, which is part
11 of Scripps Institution of Oceanography where I work. Don't take that
12 left turn, there's a light there, but go ahead until the next light, which
13 is La Jolla Shores Drive. You'll, at this point, be on Torrey Pines Road,
14 and turn left onto La Jolla Shores Drive.

15   You'll be leaving the campus on your right. Follow La Jolla Shores
16 Drive for about a half a mile. It will snake down through an S-curve
17 until the road runs parallel to the ocean, and you'll see the Pacific in
18 front of you. As soon as you come out of the S-curve, which will be
19 just after some tennis courts, look to your left for a gray building
20 called Nierenberg Hall. There's a very prominent sign "Nierenberg
21 Hall" on the building itself.

22   Turn left off La Jolla Shores Drive into the parking lot and park
23 there, and then remember to get a parking permit. Find my office.

24   Take the elevator to the fourth floor; the building is a long rectangle.

25   Go to the southwest corner of the fourth floor—that's the top floor—

26   look for room number 430, and you'll find in that room Carolyn

27   Baxter, my administrative assistant. Ask her for a parking permit, go

28   back down put the permit on your car, go back up to the office, and

29   then I'll have a cup of coffee ready for you. Thanks.

_____

_____

_____

_____

_____

_____

_____

_____

_____

_____

_____

_____

_____

_____

Study Questions

1. What is the purpose of this translation? How much time do you estimate you will need to translate this passage? What is the function of the text?

   _____

   _____

2. Describe your level of competence in the source and target languages. What is your level of competence with regard to the subject matter? With regard to methodological competence which words will you need to look up? Do you need to solve any special linguistic problems?

   _____

   _____

   _____

3. Find the main idea of the text and write it in one sentence.

   _____

   _____

   _____

4. What is the risk of error in this passage? What does this risk depend on? What is the risk of loss? What does this risk depend on?

   _____

   _____

   _____

5. Refer back to the list of considerations in this unit and write down an estimate of how much time you think you will need to complete a translation of this passage. Now complete your translation, keeping track of how long it actually takes you. Write down the difference between the estimated time and the actual time that it took to translate the passage.

_____

_____

_____

_____

Five-Step Follow-up

Complete the study questions and translation before you do the follow-up.

Step 1   **Observation**

Review your work.

Step 2   **Selection**

Underline or otherwise indicate the portions of your translation that are most satisfactory and circle any portions of the source text that you were unable to translate. With regard to the circled portions, could you translate those sections with additional preparation?

_____

_____

Step 3   **Analysis**

Analyze your overview and then the translation. Was your preparation complete? One way to analyze your translation for accuracy is by comparing the message conveyed by the source language with the message conveyed by the target language. List the propositions in the source and target language in the second and third paragraphs in space provided and compare them for meaning.

_____

_____

_____

_____

Step 4   Assessment

Assess the preparation phase and then the translation itself. How did the preparation phase help?

Step 5   Action

Develop a plan for action based on your analysis and assessment.

In the fifth step you review what you have discovered about your work in steps 1 through 4 and write the steps you would like to take to improve your performance. A suggested activity is to discuss the preparation phase with a peer and compare similarities and differences

Progress Tracking Sheet

Use this sheet to track your progress with the exercises you have completed. After performing each exercise (one or two times), answering the study questions, and doing the follow-up, fill in the tracking sheet. Note the date that you completed the exercise and give an indication of your level of accomplishment. You can use either a quantitative or a qualitative approach to track your progress.

Exercise Number	Date	First Performance	Study Questions	Follow-up Activity	Questions and Reminders	Date	Second Performance
Exercise 1.1 Quantitative Qualitative							
Exercise 1.2 Quantitative Qualitative							
Exercise 1.3 Quantitative Qualitative							
Quantitative Totals							

UNIT 2

Analyzing the Meaning of the Text

Introduction

After completing the preparation phase, you can begin analyzing the meaning of the source message as best as you can with your current resources and skill level. You must understand the source message before you can translate. The most basic level of analysis occurs when you consider the entire source language text to get the gist or overall meaning. The text can be viewed as a whole, a grouping of ideas or sentences, and grouping of words. In this unit we explore aspects of analyzing the text at these three levels.

We briefly look at Gile's two-stage model of translation and Nida and Tabor's three-stage model and apply these models to analysis at the text, idea unit, and word levels. The approaches vary, but theorists generally agree that the translator should start with the big picture and work toward the details. In psycholinguistic terms, this approach is called *top-down processing,* which is another way of saying that it is important to start with the largest amount of information possible and work down to the details. The opposite approach is *bottom-up processing,* which means that you start with the smallest units of information and work up to the whole picture. The translation process is not really unidirectional (from the big picture to the small details) or linear. The various stages of the process interact as you render the translation. For example, you form an idea about the meaning of the text, translate part of it, see if the translation makes sense, and then revise as you go along. There are three types of analysis described here and they are separated for purpose of discussion.

Analysis of the Text as a Whole

It is neccessary to analyze the source language message carefully. The approaches summarized here are not a set of rules. Kussmaul (1995) cautions against rigidly or arbitrarily following translation rules. "Apart from grammar and some very closely defined cases of conventionality, one should be very careful about talking of rules in translation. Rules should be replaced with strategies which are based on considerations of the function of utterances within situations and cultures" (p. 70). By examining several theorists' views you can build your own set of personal strategies to use in analyzing texts as a part of the translation process.

Gile's Model

As discussed in Unit 1, Gile (1995) proposes a two-stage model of translation that is easy to grasp. It consists of *comprehension* and *reformulation*. In this model analysis takes place in the comprehension stage while you assign a temporary meaning to the amount of text that you are working with.

Gile describes the amount of text that the translator works with in both phases of his model as the *translation unit*. The translation unit can be a single word, a sentence, or a larger piece of text. In order to analyze the message the translator assigns a *meaning hypothesis* to the translation unit. This means that the translator assigns a meaning to the text based on prior knowledge, linguistic abilities, and context. If the translator does not have enough prior knowledge, additional information must be sought. A critical examination of the plausibility of the meaning hypothesis in the context of other available information is the next step. If the meaning hypothesis makes sense the translator can go on to the next translation unit, if not, another hypothesis must be drawn and examined. Analysis of the sourse message is an integral and ongoing part of the translation process.

Nida and Tabor's Model

Nida and Tabor's (1982) classic model of translation includes three stages; analysis, transfer, and restructuring. They suggest that analyzing the source message depends on first getting the overall meaning, analyzing phrases to reduce ambiguity, and then analyzing the individual words. After analysis the message can be transferred to the target language and restructured in that language.

Aspects of Analysis

This section explores the analysis of function, context, word order, and ambiguity. As we saw in Unit 1, the source text has a communicative function and all the words and phrases that make up the text must be considered within the cultural framework and function of the text. Snell-Hornby (1995) writes, "For the translator, the text is not purely a linguistic phenomenon, but must also be seen in terms of its communicative function, as a unit embedded in a given situation and as part of a broader sociocultural background" (p.69). She explains that the point of analysis at this level is to trace the "web of relationships" between individual items determined by their position and role in the text, not simply the meanings of the words.

As we analyze individual expressions or sentences, we must maintain an awareness of the overall context of the source text. At the same time we must be aware that "there are some expressions that have functions only in the source language community and will have no communicative purpose in the target language community" (Kussmaul, 1995). This means that there may be some parts of the source text that we could translate into the target language but these passages would have no real meaning or function in the target language. For example, English descriptions of sound or music have no real relevance to profoundly deaf ASL users who have been deaf all their lives.

The translator must be aware of the context of the source message. Various linguists have described aspects of context with terms like "scenes," "frames," and "schema." There is debate within the field of linguistics on this subject. For a review of the various viewpoints see Metzger (2000). For our purposes in developing analysis skills in translation, we can find and use a simple approach to help us understand the importance of context and have a way to talk about it.

Translation theorists who write about text analysis cite the work of a linguist named Charles Fillmore (1977). Kussmaul (1995) explains that the Fillmore's scenes and frames theory is based in an individual's experiences of the world and on the individual's experience of the text being read or heard. He says that words and phrases are the *frames* and that the frames activate *scenes* that are like mental pictures in the mind of the reader. These scenes have been activated by these words before or have been experienced before. In this context, frames or words do not have meaning apart from the scene.

Snell-Hornby (1995) also comments on Fillmore's contribution and stresses the interaction between scenes and frames. The scene is the situation and the frame is the linguistic coding. Scenes and frames continually interact with each other. "A particular linguistic form evokes associations which themselves evoke further associations" (p.80). As a translator, you must be aware of the scenes and frames that affect the message and that the scenes and frames constantly affect each other. For example, the images evoked in your mind by the words "our vacation at the beach" may rely on general memories. Specific terms like "sand dunes," "beach umbrella," and "surf board" evoke aspects of the scene. Likewise the overall scene activates specific vocabulary associated with the beach experience, in both the translator and the audience.

Another level of analysis is examining the source message for word order and ambiguity. Word order is a consideration when working to analyze sentences for translation. The order of words in a sentence helps to construct the meaning. The sentence "Sue saw John" has the same meaning as "John was seen by Sue." However, a different meaning is conveyed if the words are rearranged in this order; "John saw Sue." Some examples from Nida and Tabor (1982, pp. 36–37) emphasize the importance of relationships between words. In an example from Bible translation studies below, the left column shows the source text and the right column one way that the source can be restated less ambiguously. Sometimes the same words are used in the ambiguous and unambiguous versions but the relationships between the words are different in each case.

Biblical phrase	*Unambiguously marked relationships*
1. the will of God	God wills
2. the God of peace	God causes/produces peace
3. the word of truth	the word is true
4. servant of all	he serves all (people)
5. the land of Judea	the land is Judea

The phrases in the right-hand column contain less ambiguity. The source language construction or arrangement of words may be ambiguous but the translator must begin with as unambiguous a statement as possible. Nida and Tabor explain that in the right hand column events are expressed as verbs, objects are expressed as nouns, and abstracts are expressed as adjectives or adverbs (p. 39). When the source text's meaning is less distorted there will be less distortion in the target text. One way to reduce possible distortion of the meaning is to paraphrase the source text before beginning the transfer process. The exercises in this unit provide practice in paraphrasing the source text before translating.

The information in this unit emphasize the importance of analysis in translation. It is important for the translator to consider the text as a whole before establishing a meaning hypothesis for an individual translation unit within the text. Understanding how scenes and frames can affect the translation process can improve the translation. After practicing with the exercises in this unit you will see that even the simplest text can evoke a wide variety of scenes in individuals. If the translator is aware that scenes depend on prior experiences, then the translator can render a translation that takes into account the fact that no two scenes will be exactly alike and as a result no two translations will be exactly alike.

Analysis of Words

There are many aspects of analysis at the word level. Some of the broadest and most useful are summarized here. Nida and Tabor suggest that after analyzing relationships between words, it is important to study the various meanings of words. Analysis at the word level gives you an opportunity to be sure that you have correctly understood all the words in the source message.

There are several reasons why you might have trouble at this level. Kussmaul (1995) says that you may not know the word or its meaning, or you may know the word but not understand its usage in the current context, or the word may be used in an idiosyncratic way by the author. When a word is used in an idiosyncratic way, you can infer the meaning from the context, but you may not be entirely sure of the meaning. You can consult dictionaries, books on English usage, and a thesaurus to help you understand the meanings of words. You can also talk with native users of English to obtain more information about how specific words are used in specific contexts. For example, common words like "bit" and "bus" have different meanings in a technical, computer-based setting than they do in a nontechnical setting. As a translator you must explore all the possible meanings of the words in the text and select the one that is most appropriate to the current context.

Larson (1987) explains that the most difficult task facing the translator is that of finding lexical equivalents when objects and events are not known in the target culture. "The lack of lexical equivalents may be due to differences in geography, customs, beliefs, worldview, level of technological development or similar factors."

The concept of hierarchical relationships between words is important for interpreters. Nida and Tabor (1982) explain that *taxonomies* are systems of classification that show the relationship between words. They point out that "animal" is more inclusive than "mammal," "mammal" is more inclusive than "dog," and "dog" is more inclusive than "terrier." This sample taxonomy goes from more general to more specific. It is important to know which words are general and which are more specific. In the process of translating you may not be able to find a word in the target language that is as specific or as general as the one in the source language. Analyze the word in the target language to see if it adequately conveys the concept intended in the source language and whether it is more general or more specific. Sometimes the target language word does not contain the same level of specificity or generality.

When you must choose a more general or more specific word or expression the risk of error and loss is increased. Nida and Tabor point out that some languages will have a general term for a concept while other languages have a variety of specific words to convey the same concept, but not a general term. The opposite can also be true. For example, in English, the terms "furniture," "fruit," and "vegetable" all are general, while "chair," "apple," and "squash" are more specific. It is possible that the language you are translating into will have different levels of specificity that your translation must accommodate. A careful analysis will help you determine the level of specificity you can attain in the target language.

This unit has explored the importance of analyzing the function, context, word order, ambiguity, and meaning of words. When you take time to analyze the source text at these levels you are on your way to creating a faithful translation.

Analyzing the Meaning Exercises

EXERCISE 2.1

The Phone Call
DIANA GORMAN

Directions

Find and watch this selection on your videotape. Write a description of the audience in the space provided. Stop the tape and read the transcript of *The Phone Call*. Answer the study questions. Translate the passages into the target language. If you are working into a signed language, first write the translation in gloss form and then videotape a signed version of this passage. If you are working into a written language, write your translation in the space provided below the passage. After you complete your translation do the follow-up.

_____

_____

Transcript for *The Phone Call,* by Diana Gorman

1   A woman is looking for a phone number in the phone book. She is

2   dialing the phone number. She is talking on the phone.

_____

_____

_____

Study Questions

1. Read the entire passage to get the gist. Do the speaker's words (frames) activate a mental scene? Describe the scene in as much detail as possible.

_____

_____

2. Formulate a meaning hypothesis for each sentence. Paraphrase the sentences in the transcript. This means you rewrite the sentences in English. You may change the order of information within the phrases as long as the meaning is held constant. Does the meaning expressed in the paraphrase support your meaning hypothesis?

    _____

    _____

    _____

3. Check each word in the transcript to see if it can be made more specific or more general in English without changing the meaning. List the possibilities for any word that you find that can be made more general or more specific.

    _____

    _____

    _____

4. Is there a more general way to say "phone number"? Would the translation of the more general term be the same as or different than the translation of the more specific term? Would the communicative effect of both translations be the same?

    _____

    _____

5   The speaker uses the word "she." Who does the word refer to? If you are working into ASL or another signed language, how do you analyze "talk on the phone?" How do you analyze this concept if you know that the woman is deaf and using a telecommunications device for the deaf?

    _____

    _____

Five-Step Follow-up

Complete the study questions and translation before you do the follow-up.

Step 1   Observation

Review your responses to all parts of the exercise that you have done so far.

Step 2   Selection

Circle the number of any study questions you had difficulty answering. Underline any portion of the source text that you had difficulty translating.

Step 3   Analysis

Were your meaning hypotheses accurate? After analysis did the passage still have the same meaning as it did when you first considered the entire text? How did analysis at the phrase and word level reinforce the meaning hypothesis? Determine your accuracy in analysis by comparing the source and target language to see if the message is preserved.

_____

_____

Step 4   Assessment

Assess your ability to use analysis as a means to prepare to translate. Write a sentence that states how analyzing the source text affects your decisions in the translation process.

_____

_____

Step 5   Action

Develop a plan for action based on your analysis and assessment.

In the fifth step you review what you have discovered about your work in steps 1 through 4 and write the steps you would like to take to improve your use of analysis as a part of the translation process. For example, select a passage from another unit in this workbook and analyze the passage at the grammatical level and word level before translating it.

_____

_____

EXERCISE 2.2

Watching TV
DIANA GORMAN

Directions

Find and watch this selection on your videotape. Write a description of the audience in the space provided. Stop the tape and read the transcript of *Watching TV*. Answer the study questions. Translate the passage into the target language. If you are working into a signed language, first write the translation in gloss form and then videotape a signed version of this passage. If you are working into a written language write your translation in the space provided below the passage. After completing the translation, do the follow-up.

_____

_____

Transcript for *Watching TV,* by Diana Gorman

1 A man is looking through his TV guide. He turns on the TV and there is

2 static. He finds his TV show and then he sits down and enjoys the show.

_____

_____

_____

Study Questions

1. Read the entire passage to get the gist. Do the speaker's words (frames) activate a mental scene? Describe the scene in as much detail as possible.

_____

_____

2. Formulate a meaning hypothesis for each sentence. Paraphrase the sentences in the transcript. This means you rewrite the sentences in English. You may change the order of information within the phrases as long as the meaning is held constant. Does the meaning expressed in the paraphrase support your original meaning hypothesis?

    _____

    _____

    _____

    _____

3. Check each word in the transcript to see if it can be made more specific or more general without changing the meaning. List the possibilities for any word that you find that can be made more general or more specific.

    _____

    _____

4. The speaker says "…and there is static.' How do you use hypothesis testing to help determine the meaning of this phrase? Look for examples of ambiguity in the entire selection and write them in the space provided and then rewrite any ambiguous phrases in a nonambiguous way.

    _____

    _____

    _____

    _____

5. The speaker uses the word "static." Do you know how to translate this word into the target language? If not, look up "static" in a dictionary to find the meaning in English and then consult a thesaurus to find synonyms for "static." You may find more than one meaning. Which one is appropriate for this context?

_____

_____

Five-Step Follow-up

Complete the study questions and translation before you do the follow-up.

Step 1   **Observation**

Review your responses to all parts of the exercise that you have done so far.

Step 2   **Selection**

Circle the number of any study questions you had difficulty answering. Underline any portion of the source text that you had difficulty translating.

Step 3   **Analysis**

Were your meaning hypotheses accurate? After analysis did the passage still have the same meaning as it did when you first considered the entire text? How did analysis at the phrase and word level reinforce the meaning hypothesis? Determine your accuracy in analysis by comparing the source and target language to see if the message is preserved.

_____

_____

_____

Step 4   **Assessment**

Assess your ability to use analysis as a way to prepare to translate. This exercise was not more complex than the first one in this unit. Write a sentence stating how analyzing the source text affects your decisions in the translation process.

_____

_____

Step 5   **Action**

Review what you have discovered about your work in steps 1 through 4 and make some decisions about what steps you would like to take to improve your use of analysis as a part of the translation process. For example, select a passage from another unit in this workbook and analyze the passage at the grammatical level and word level before translating it. Write a plan for action based on your analysis and assessment.

_____

_____

EXERCISE 2.3

Directions to Deep Creek
DAVID BURNIGHT

Directions

Find and watch this selection on your videotape. Write a description of the audience in the space provided. Stop the tape and read the transcript of *Directions to Deep Creek*. Answer the study questions. Translate the passage into the target language. If you are working into a signed language, first write the translation in gloss form and then videotape a signed version of this passage. If you are working into a written language, write your translation in the space provided below the passage. Complete the follow-up.

_____

_____

Transcript for *Directions to Deep Creek* by David Burnight

1 Hi, my name is David Burnight, and I'm going to give you directions

2 on how to get to Deep Creek, in case you ever want to go to Deep

3 Creek. Well, first you go up to the county road and you turn right

4 and you go about a mile to where the pavement ends. And then

5 you're on a dirt road with many little winding turns and it's a good

6 idea to honk your horn before you go around any curve, because you

7 can't see anybody who's coming. It's also a good idea to wait if there's

8   a car ahead of you, because they'll raise a lot of dust on the dirt road.

9   And it's a good idea to not get into the ruts—just to follow along on

10   the high parts of the road. After you've gone down the hill a ways

11   you'll come to a creek and cross over, and there's a homestead cabin

12   on the right and just past the homestead cabin there are two

13   possibilities: the road forks off to the right, and if you take that right

14   fork and go about a quarter of a mile or so, pretty soon the creek will

15   be visible right on your left. And you can go to the very sharp right

16   turn and park. You have to park there, because if you go much

17   farther the road is all washed out. And you can go down to the creek

18   there, and there's a pool that's five feet deep with a slide in it, and

19   some rocks that you can lie out on—very pretty.

20   The other possibility is to go, instead of taking that right fork, is

21   to go straight ahead and cross another creek and ignore the road to

22   Squint's ranch over on the left, and go straight ahead to a very steep

23   downhill. And it's kind of scary but actually you can do it alright in

24   your car. At the bottom of the hill there's another creek to cross and

25   then you drive about a quarter of a mile through the woods along a

26   dirt road and you'll come to a parking lot. There may be one or two

27   other cars there, maybe more on a weekend. This is a favorite place

28   for fishermen and for picnickers and if you go down the path toward

29   the creek, cross over the little creek on your left on a log, and walk

30   along the path about 50 feet you'll come to a big bridge—a hiker's

31   bridge. And you can either go under the bridge or go up and cross

32   over the bridge and you'll find a big pool to swim in and a sandy

33   beach. It's a lovely spot and I hope you find it.

_____

_____

_____

_____

_____

_____

_____

_____

_____

_____

_____

_____

_____

_____

_____

_____

_____

_____

_____

_____

_____

_____

_____

_____

_____

Study Questions

1. Read the entire passage to get the gist. Do the speaker's words (frames) activate a mental scene? Describe the scene in as much detail as possible.

    _____

    _____

    _____

    _____

2. Use your analysis skills to formulate a meaning hypothesis for the portions of the transcript below. Paraphrase the excerpts from the transcript. This means you rewrite the sentences in English using different words or word order while preserving the meaning. You may change the order of information within the phrases as long as the meaning is held constant. Does the meaning expressed in the paraphrase support the meaning hypothesis?

    a. Well, first you go up to the *county* road and you turn right and you go about a mile to where the pavement ends.

    _____

    _____

    _____

    b. ...and it's a good idea to honk your horn before you go around any curve, because you can't *see anybody who's coming*

    _____

    _____

_____

_____

c. It's also a good idea to wait if there's a car ahead of you, because they'll raise a lot of dust on the dirt road.

_____

_____

_____

_____

d. And it's a good idea to not get into the ruts—just to follow along on the high parts of the road.

_____

_____

_____

e. After you've gone down the hill a ways you'll come to a creek and cross over,

_____

_____

_____

_____

f. and there's a _homestead cabin_ on the right and just past the homestead cabin there are two possibilities: the road forks off to the right, and if you take that right fork and go about a quarter of a mile or so, pretty soon the creek will be visible right on your left.

_____

_____

_____

_____

_____

_____

_____

g. And you can go to the very sharp right turn and park.

_____

_____

h. And you can go down to the creek there.

_____

_____

i. The other possibility is to go, instead of taking that right fork, is to go straight ahead and cross another creek and ignore the road to Squint's ranch over on the left, and go straight ahead to a very steep downhill.

_____

_____

_____

_____

_____

_____

j. And it's kind of scary but actually you can do it alright in your car.

_____

_____

k. At the bottom of the hill there's another creek to cross and then you drive about a quarter of a mile through the woods along a dirt road and you'll come to a parking lot. There may be one or two other cars there, maybe more on a weekend.

_____

_____

_____

_____

_____

_____

_____

l. This is a favorite place for fishermen and for picnickers and if you go down the path toward the creek, cross over the little creek on your left on a log, and walk along the path about 50 feet you'll come to a big bridge—a hiker's bridge.

_____

_____

_____

_____

_____

_____

_____

_____

m. And you can either go under the bridge or go up and cross over the bridge and you'll find a big pool to swim in and a sandy beach. It's a lovely spot and I hope you find it.

_____

_____

_____

_____

_____

3. The following words are taken from the transcript of *Directions to Deep Creek*. Find a synonym for each. Is the synonym appropriate for the context?

rocks   _____

creek   _____

hill   _____

Squint's ranch   _____

dirt road   _____

4. Analyze the following sentence.

    "It's also a good idea to wait if there's a car ahead of you, because they'll raise a lot of dust on the dirt road."

    What does the word "wait" mean in this context? What does "they'll" refer to?

    _____

    _____

5. Analyze the following sentence.

    "The other possibility is to go, instead of taking that right fork, is to go straight ahead and cross another creek and ignore the road to Squint's ranch over on the left, and go straight ahead to a very steep downhill."

    What does "the other possibility" refer to? The speaker says you "cross another creek" but does not say that there is a bridge. What information about the crossing will show up in your translation? How can you make the "road to Squint's ranch" more general?

    _____

    _____

    _____

    _____

    "The other possibility"

    "cross another creek"

    "the road to Squint's ranch"

Five-Step Follow-up

Complete the study questions and translation before you do the follow-up.

Step 1   Observation

Review your responses to all parts of the exercise that you have done so far.

Step 2   Selection

Circle the number of any study questions you had difficulty answering. Underline any portions of the source text that you had difficulty translating.

Step 3   Analysis

Were your meaning hypotheses accurate? After analysis did the passage still have the same meaning as it did when you first considered the entire text? How did analysis at the phrase and word level reinforce the meaning hypothesis? Determine your accuracy in analysis by comparing the source and target language to see if the message is preserved.

_____

_____

_____

Step 4   Assessment

Assess your ability to use analysis as a way to prepare your translation. This exercise was more complex than the previous two but you should still have a sense of how your analysis of the source text affects your decisions in the translation process. Write a brief description of how analysis helped you translate.

_____

_____

_____

Step 5.   Action

Review what you have discovered about your work in steps 1 through 4 and make some decisions about what steps you would like to take to improve your use of analysis as a part of the translation process. For example, consider other selections in this workbook and practice your analysis skills. Write your plan of action.

_____

_____

Progress Tracking Sheet

Use this sheet to track your progress with the exercises you have completed. After performing each exercise (one or two times), answering the study questions, and doing the follow-up, fill in the tracking sheet. Note the date that you completed the exercise and give an indication of your level of accomplishment. You can use either a quantitative or a qualitative approach to track your progress.

Exercise Number	Date	First Performance	Study Questions	Follow-up Activity	Questions and Reminders	Date	Second Performance
Exercise 2.1 Quantitative Qualitative							
Exercise 2.2 Quantitative Qualitative							
Exercise 2.3 Quantitative Qualitative							
Quantitative Totals							

UNIT
3

Message Transfer

Introduction

Despite the fact that it is not visible, the transfer stage is the heart of the translation process. During the transfer process, the source language message is mentally rendered into the form of the target language. The transfer process does not include the actual writing of the translation or any visible rendition of the translation. This unit discusses ways that the translator can affect the translation, the importance of temporal, spatial, and logical relations, visualization, form and meaning, and loss during transfer.

How the Translator Affects the Translation

The translator must be aware of the many ways in which he or she can affect the translation. The translator's linguistic and translation skills, prior knowledge, and bias can affect the translation. The final version of the translation is the product of analysis, transfer, and reformulation. Weaknesses in any of these three areas will affect the translation and its impact on the target audience.

Bias in Translation

Nida and Tabor (1982) explain that it is likely that each translator has unconscious biases about at least three variables: the subject matter, the source language, and the target language. The first variable these authors discuss suggests that the translator can sometimes know too much about the subject matter. It is not the knowledge or lack of knowledge of the subject matter that is the issue here. Instead, it is the lack of *imagination* that can cause problems. As a translator, you must not assume that your intended audience has the same depth of understanding of the subject that you have. It is important to imagine the level of understanding of the audience and to realize the implications of that level of understanding for the translation you render. This kind of imagination asks you to project what could logically be true about the audience and their knowledge of the subject. You must use logic in addition to intuition to avoid fabricating information about the audience. Also, it is possible that a translator could have false ideas or information about a subject. When that happens, bias is even more likely because the translator will not be aware of the discrepancy between what they believe to be true about the subject and the facts. Keep in mind that the way you feel or think about a topic can influence how you translate the text.

The second variable that can affect bias is the translator's skill in his or her first language. Nida and Tabor suggest that sometimes translators are insecure about their first language. According to these authors this insecurity expresses itself in two different ways. One is that translators "feel obliged to imitate the forms of other languages which they regard as having more prestige." These translators "borrow wholesale, not only words, idioms, and stylistic devices, but also grammatical forms, for they conclude that these prestigious languages must be right" (p.101). This kind of wholesale importing of English features into the target language often appears in the work of translators and interpreters working into ASL. It is less clear whether borrowing English features is due to lack of competence in ASL or if it is due to the unconscious reasons Nida and Tabor suggest. The second way that insecurity about your own first language may express itself is in an exaggerated confidence when, in fact, competence is lacking. Nida and Tabor suggest that this is a "superiority reaction to insecurity." The results of any kind of insecurity in the source language are equally disastrous for the translation because this insecurity leads to distortion of the message.

The third variable is the translator's competence in the target language when the target language is the translator's second language. When the target language is the interpreter's second language target language competence is often an area of weakness in translation as well as in interpretation. Ideally, the translator or interpreter has had advanced language study in their second language in order to overcome weaknesses. Even so, these weaknesses tend to appear. Using a peer reviewer or working on back-translation skills can lessen this variable's affect.

Nida and Tabor propose that the translator can affect the transfer stage by being ignorant of the translation process. It is important to realize that translation is not simply replacing words in one language with words from another language. These authors say that historically the focus in translation has been placed on the word and later on the sentence. "Expert translators and linguists have been able to demonstrate that the individual sentence in turn is not enough. The focus should be on the paragraph, and to some extent the total discourse" (p. 102). Nida and Tabor go on to explain that if you do not look at the entire passage or text before beginning the translation, you will miss the transitions and connections between parts of the text. Nida and Tabor emphasize that it is important to consider the entire text while translating its component parts because the parts must fit together to form a single unit.

It is important to evaluate your skills honestly. If you identify the ways your particular knowledge and skills affect a translation, you can work to ensure that the translation is not adversely affected.

Transfer in Translation

Since transfer is not visible and cannot be measured directly, we can only know about the transfer process by studying its outcomes in the translation. If we compare the source language and target language versions and find that they do not convey the same message, then we can say that the problem lies in one of three broad categories, competence in the source language, competence in the target language, or competence in the transfer process. If the problem is one of competence in the transfer process it means that the translator has a good enough command of both languages but does not know how to accurately convey the message from one language to another.

If you are a novice, you may wonder how you can test your own translation to see if the message is preserved. To some extent, while you are in training you can rely on your teachers to help you see if your translation preserves the meaning. In daily practice as a professional, you must be able to make your own determinations about the faithfulness of your translations. If you are unable to decide if your translation captures the meaning of the original, it will be due to weaknesses in either source or target language competence or in the translation process itself. Unit 6 in this workbook deals with testing the translation in more depth. Remember that in this unit we focus on transfer, but because transfer is invisible, we must look at the translation (product) and make inferences about transfer.

Remember that translation is not really a linear sequence of discreet steps. It is a dynamic process. The preparation phase affects analysis, which interacts with transfer, which affects reformulation, which can lead to a reanalysis. During the translation process, the emphasis shifts continuously through analysis and reformulating by moving back and forth between these two as you work through the transfer phase. Nida and Tabor (1982) say that you must not only deal at the level of idea units, but must also work to "back up" to the point where you see the relevance of these idea units to the entire discourse. They suggest that there are three types of relations between idea units that you should keep in mind: (1) temporal, (2) spatial and, (3) logical.

Being aware of temporal relationships between idea units allows you to arrange the idea units into an appropriate time sequence. Nida and Tabor point out that temporal relations permit you to include the notion of several events that happen at the same time or events that span a long period of time. An example of a type of discourse that relies on careful translation of temporal events is directions. Driving directions depend on the sequence of events being presented in a specific order. Directions for cooking require that certain ingredients be added before others. In either of these examples, if the temporal order is not preserved in the target language, the message will be skewed. This aspect of the transfer process becomes especially important when working into languages that order time-based events in a structure differently than does the source language.

Spatial relationships allow for two different possibilities. "One is between objects such as a house and a tree, and the other is the spatial relationship between the viewer and other objects" (Nida and Tabor, 1982). Spatial relationships point out the importance of the text's point of view, who is speaking, and where that speaker is in relation to the things being talked about. Spatial relations are especially important in visual languages like ASL. In ASL it is important to establish the location of the objects and people referred to in the signing space. The signer must establish whether the objects being referred to are in view or not and must be consistent in referring to those objects and their relative locations in space.

A valuable tool for developing skill in preserving spatial relationships is visualization. Visualization skills allow you to imagine where people are in relation to each other or to objects. For example, a text may refer to a person speaking to a woman and giving her a pen although the text may not reveal which person is to the right and which is to the left, if one is standing behind the other, or if they are facing each other. If you are working into a visual language, you must establish the people and objects in locations in space and then refer back to them systematically and repeatedly. If you do not know the actual location of the objects or people you must visualize them. Use the visualization as a point of reference until the actors or objects shift locations. Use hypothesis testing to establish locations until you find evidence of actual locations.

Visualization skills play an important role during transfer for interpreters of spoken languages and signed language. If you can envision in your mind's eye where the people and objects are located, then you can work from the visualization into the target language. In the next unit you will practice actually assigning locations to objects and people if you are working into a signed language. In this unit, practice visualizing relative locations whether they are explicitly stated or not.

Logical relations are a third type of relations that Nida and Tabor discuss. Logical relations refer to "cause and effect or condition and consequence." Languages may differ in how they arrange cause and effect clauses, such as the if-then clause in English. For example, the English sentence "if it is on sale, then I will buy it" may be expressed in the following structure in ASL: SUPPOSE COST REDUCE, I BUY. As stated in the Introduction to Translating from English, the ASL surface structure is represented in all capital letters to indicate that these English words are simply symbols, or glosses, for the signs that are used in ASL, which does not have a written form. This comparison between English and ASL demonstrates that the languages express cause and effect in very different ways. During transfer you must keep temporal, spatial, and logical relationships in mind.

Form and Meaning

Before beginning the transfer process, it is important to review the distinctions between form and meaning. According to Nida and Tabor, "the form is the external shape of the message" or the actual words used. The meaning is the "conceptual intent of the message" (1982, p. 105). For additional information and practice in clarifying the distinction between form and meaning, please see *The Effective Interpreting Series: English Skills Development.* When translating from one language to another you must convey the meaning in a form that is appropriate to the target language. The form of the source and target languages are different. Nida and Tabor say that this concept can be visualized by imagining that you have two very different shaped suitcases. In order to pack your clothes in the first suitcase you must fold and pack them in a certain way. To pack the same clothes in the other suitcase you must fold them and pack them in an entirely different way. The external shapes of the two suitcases can be very different even though the clothes in each suitcase are the same clothes. In this analogy the clothes represent the message and the suitcases represent the source language and the target language.

Loss during Transfer

The transfer process naturally includes some type of "loss" of content. Nida and Tabor suggest that some of the most common areas of loss occur in the translations of figurative language such as idioms. Idioms are one type of figurative language that have a surface structure or form that does not reveal the meaning. For example, the phrase to "let the cat out of the bag" has nothing to do with cats or bags, instead, it means to tell a secret or disclose some information. According to Nida and Tabor there are three considerations to keep in mind when translating idioms. One is to find an idiom in the target language that is nearly equivalent in meaning to the source language idiom. A second approach to translating idioms is to find a nonidiomatic way to express the concept in the target language. By using one of these two approaches you can avoid loss when translating.

The third consideration involves instances where a nonidiomatic expression can be expressed as an idiom in the target language.

The same approaches used when working with idioms can be used with other forms of figurative language. Loss can occur if you are not aware that an expression is figurative and do not know that expression's relationship to a more literal view of the same concept. For example, if you do not know that "don't let the cat out of the bag" is an idiom, you might convey a message that says, "keep the cat in a bag" instead of an admonition to keep some information secret. After analyzing the source language for meaning, the next step is to paraphrase the source, and then translate the paraphrase. For example, if the figurative expression in the source language is "I am keeping my eye on you" you can first paraphrase it to "I am watching you closely." It is more common to translate a figurative expression as nonfigurative expression but there are times when a nonfigurative word may be paraphrased using figurative language and then translated.

Since transfer is a mental process, to do it effectively requires discipline and training. The discussions in Units 1 and 2 highlighted some of the linguistic and technical skills that you must use during transfer. At the same time, there are things that you should avoid doing in order to enhance the transfer process. It is especially important to avoid negative self-talk, such as "I should have a better command of verb conjugations or classifiers," or " my translation will probably be the weakest in the group." Negative self-talk diverts you from the transfer process and is not productive.

The transfer process allows you to formulate a translation in your mind before committing that translation to paper or videotape. There are many aspects of transfer. Some of the basic considerations have been included in this unit. For more detail and other ideas regarding the transfer process in translation, refer to Chapter 6 in Nida and Tabor's *The Theory and Practice of Translation (1982)*.

Message Transfer Exercises

EXERCISE 3.1

The Refreshment Stand
DIANA GORMAN

Directions

Find and watch this selection on your tape. Write a description of the audience in the space provided. Stop the tape and refer to the printed transcript.

Translate the passage. If you are working into a signed language, videotape your translation. Start by visualizing the relative locations of the actors and objects in the text. While you are translating, be aware of what is occurring in your mind as you go through the transfer process. Pay close attention to your thought process during transfer. After you complete the translation, answer the study questions and do the follow-up.

_____

_____

Transcript for *The Refreshment Stand,* by Diana Gorman

1   A little boy goes up to an ice cream stand. He gives the woman behind

2   the counter his money and she gives him some ice cream. He happily

3   walks along eating his ice cream.

4   When the ice cream is gone, he throws the stick in a trash can.

_____

_____

_____

_____

_____

_____

Study Questions

1. Write a brief summary of your thought processes during transfer. Did you have questions in your mind about how to translate the passage? If so write the questions. Did your thoughts include any negative self-talk or commentary about the text that was unrelated to the translation process? If so write what you were thinking. Do you mentally try out various translations and settle on one? Do you find alternatives easily?

_____

_____

_____

_____

2. If you have prior knowledge or experience with buying ice cream at a refreshment stand, then it may be easy for you to translate these sentences. Imagine that you are translating these sentences for a person who has never purchased ice cream from a refreshment stand. How will this knowledge of your audience affect your translation?

_____

_____

_____

_____

3. Look for bias in your work by examining your source language competence. Examine your target language competence with regard to these sentences. Is your translation grammatically appropriate to the target language? Do you have any biases regarding either of your languages or the subject matter? If your translation follows English word order instead of the word order of the target language that may represent a bias in favor of English, or it may represent lack of competence in the target language, either of which can negatively affect the translation.

_____

_____

_____

_____

4. Check your translation to see if the temporal relations have been held constant in the transfer process.

_____

_____

_____

_____

5. Did you use visualization to help you establish the spatial relations in the text? If so how did that help? If not, go back and visualize all the information. Were you able to preserve the logical relations? Remember this means that the cause and effect relationships are preserved. If you have questions about how to preserve these relations, write them here.

_____

_____

_____

_____

Five-Step Follow-up

Step 1   Observation

Review your work with the exercises.

Step 2   Selection

Circle any source language sentences whose translations you would like to improve.

Step 3   Analysis

Describe the thought processes you used during transfer to determine relations (temporal, spatial, and logical). By examining your thought processes and the product you can see if you have dealt appropriately with any idioms, figurative terms, or general and specific terms.

_____

_____

_____

_____

Step 4   Assessment

Review your translations and your answers to the study questions and note how your translation is affected by an awareness of the transfer process. You have learned several new translation techniques. Check whether you have mastered the new techniques involved in developing insight into the transfer process, checking your work for biases in terms of the topic and languages involved, relations within the text, and idioms, figurative language and general/specific concepts. If you notice problems in any of these areas or have questions about the transfer process, write them here.

_____

_____

_____

_____

Step 5   Action

Write a plan for action based on your analysis and assessment. Review what you have discovered about your work in steps 1 through 4 and write the steps you would like to take to improve your performance. Look at your answer to step 4 to find where you can take action. For example, you may wish to concentrate on awareness of possible linguistic biases or problems with spatial relations when you approach another practice translation. Or you may wish to practice translating idioms. Consult a dictionary of idioms to help you understand the meanings of idioms.

_____

_____

_____

_____

EXERCISE 3.2

Bathing the Dog
DIANA GORMAN

Directions

Find and listen to this selection on your tape. Write a description of the audience in the space provided. Stop the tape and refer to the printed transcript. Translate the passage. If you are working into a signed language, videotape your translation. Start by visualizing the relative locations of the actors and objects in the text. While you are translating, be aware of what is occurring in your mind as you go through the transfer process. Pay close attention to your thought process during transfer. After you complete the translation, answer the study questions and do the follow-up.

_____

_____

Transcript for *Bathing the Dog,* by Diana Gorman

1 A dog rolls around in the mud. A little boy and little girl scold the dog.

2 The little boy and little girl get out a swimming pool to clean the dog

3 in. They push and pull the dog to try to get him into the pool. Once

4 the dog is in the pool, they pour some water on the dog from a hose.

5 Then they lather up the dog with soap. As the little girl holds down the

6 dog, the little boy washes off the soap. Then the little girl and little boy

7 dry off the dog. The dog shakes off the water, getting the little boy and

8 little girl all wet. Now, the dog is nice and clean, but the little boy and

9 little girl are all dirty.

_____

_____

_____

_____

_____

_____

_____

_____

_____

_____

_____

Study Questions

1. Write a brief summary of your thought processes as you translated this selection. Did you have questions in your mind about how to translate the passage? If so, write the questions. Did your thoughts include any negative self-talk or commentary about the text that was unrelated to the translation process? If so, write what you were thinking. Do you mentally try out various translations and settle on one? Do you find alternatives easily?

_____

_____

_____

2. If you have prior knowledge or experience with giving a dog a bath, then it may be easy for you to translate these sentences. Imagine that you are translating these sentences for a person who has never bathed a dog. How will this knowledge of your audience affect your translation?

_____

_____

_____

_____

3. Look for bias in your work by examining your source language compe-
    tence. Examine your target language competence. Is your translation
    grammatically appropriate to the target language? Do you have any biases
    regarding either of your languages or the subject matter? If your transla-
    tion follows English word order instead of the word order of the target
    language, that may represent a bias in favor of English or it may represent
    lack of competence in the target language, either of which can negatively
    affect the translation.

_____

_____

_____

_____

4. Check your translation to see if the temporal relations have been held
    constant in the transfer process.

_____

_____

_____

_____

5. Did you use visualization to help you establish the spatial relations in the
    text? If so how did that help? If you did not use visualization, go back and
    visualize all the information. Were you able to preserve the logical rela-
    tions? Remember this means that the cause and effect relationships are
    preserved. If you have questions about how to preserve these relations,
    write them here.

_____

_____

_____

Five-Step Follow-up

Step 1   Observation

Review your responses to all three parts of the exercise that you have done so far.

Step 2   Selection

Circle any source language sentences whose translations you would like to improve.

Step 3   Analysis

Describe the thought processes you used during translation to determine relations (temporal, spatial, and logical). By examining your thought processes you can double-check that you have dealt appropriately with any idioms, figurative terms, or general and specific terms.

_____

_____

_____

_____

Step 4   Assessment

Review your translations and your answers to the study questions to note how your translation is affected by an awareness of the transfer process. You have learned several new translation techniques. Check whether you have mastered the new techniques involved in the transfer process, checking your work for biases in terms of the topic and languages involved, relations within the text, and idioms, figurative language, and general/specific concepts. If you notice problems in any of these areas or have questions about the transfer process, write them here.

_____

_____

_____

_____

Step 5   Action

Write a plan for action based on your analysis and assessment. Review what you have discovered about your work in steps 1 through 4 and write the steps you would like to take to improve your performance. Look at your answer to step 4 to find where you can take action. For example, you may wish to concentrate on awareness of temporal relations when you approach another practice translation. Or you may wish to focus on spatial relations in translations. For additional practice you can select *Directions to Deep Creek* and work on the translation again with spatial relationships in mind.

_____

_____

_____

_____

EXERCISE 3.3

The Payroll Process
JEFF HARDISON

Directions

Find and listen to this selection on your tape. Write a description of the audience in the space provided. Stop the tape and refer to the printed transcript. Translate the passage. If you are working into a signed language, videotape your translation. Start by visualizing the relative locations of the actors and objects in the text. While you are translating, be aware of what is occurring in your mind during the transfer process. After you complete the translation, answer the study questions and do the follow-up.

Transcript for *The Payroll Process,* by Jeff Hardison

1   Hello. My name is Jeff Hardison. You know, in corporate America

2   today, probably the largest single expense that any business has is its

3   payroll. So, I thought that it might be interesting to kinda talk a little

4   bit about how timecards actually get translated and become checks—

5   that process, and how it happens. It's actually less complicated than I

6   thought. I had a friend of mine, who is a CPA, kinda go through the

7   process for me.

8   What usually happens in the beginning is that you have an

9   individual who will fill out a timecard, and then that timecard has to

10 be taken to be approved by somebody who has the authority to do

11 so, typically the supervisor of whatever corporation, business, or unit

12 that we're talking about.

13   After that, then, the timecard gets submitted into the Accounting

14 Department. Now, what the Accounting Department does, at this

15 point, is they take the card, and then they pull up what they have on

16 the computer, typically, nowadays, they use computers, they pull up a

17 log of all of the employees that work there and match up numbers, to

18 ensure that, in fact, the employee is an existing employee, active,

19 because this is one of the first checks that are used in order to prevent

20 someone from trying to embezzle or illegally get money out of a

21 company that they ought not to.

22   Once that's been done, then what happens is that they then input

23 the number of hours that the individual has had into what they call

24 an "automated payroll system"—so they pull up specifically a kind of

25 program, a computer program, that you then feed in that employee's

26 number with the hours. And what's really nice about the computer

27 programs is that it will automatically do all of the tax work for you. It

28 will do the Federal Tax, it will do the State Tax, it will take care of

29 annual leave, sick leave; it will divide all of that up. And, also if you

30   have situations where, perhaps, a corporation does different jobs, it
31   will begin to actually compartmentalize which jobs were done by that
32   individual. The reason that's so much nicer now in computers is that
33   in the days before computers, that actually all had to be figured by
34   hand. You can imagine how much time that would have taken for
35   someone to have to do manually.

36   Once that's been done, then you're basically pretty much ready to
37   go and start printing the checks. What you then do, once the
38   information, as I said, has been input, is you then go through and do
39   what's called a "first edit." And what that is, is that you go back and
40   check to ensure that the inputted information that you've inputted
41   actually matches what is supposed to be there, so that you haven't
42   done something in error. Then, you go to the printer, if that's where
43   you do it, some corporations, now, do not actually print their checks
44   in their own place of business, they'll often have another corporation
45   or other business handle that, but for those that do, you would then
46   go to the printer, and then you would put your checks in, feed it into
47   the printer, and then basically hit "print." Then, all of the checks
48   come through. Then, they go through what's called the "second edit,"
49   which is basically physically looking at the checks. Now, that
50   depends, again, on the size of your corporation—if it's really huge,
51   and you're talking, you know, several hundreds or even thousands of
52   people, obviously that's not practical. But, if it's a smaller corporation
53   or business, and you can actually do that, they do what's called a
54   "second check." Or, just ensure that every check that's been printed
55   was in fact a check that needed to be, or matches up to what all of
56   the employees have done.

57   After that, someone is usually delegated to tear them apart, put
58   them into an envelope, it's distributed to everybody, and happy hour
59   hits, and everyone's happy.

_____

_____

_____

_____

_____

_____

_____

_____

_____

_____

_____

_____

_____

_____

_____

_____

_____

_____

_____

_____

_____

_____

_____

_____

_____

_____

_____

_____

_____

_____

_____

_____

_____

_____

_____

_____

_____

Study Questions

1. Write a brief summary of your thought processes during transfer. If you have prior knowledge or experience with the payroll process, then it may be easy for you to translate this passage. Imagine that you are translating for a person who has no prior experience with the payroll process. How will this knowledge of your audience affect your translation? Do you mentally try out various translations and settle on one? Do you find alternatives easily?

    _____

    _____

    _____

    _____

2. Examine your source language competence. Do you feel that you have fully understood this passage? Examine your target language competence. Is your translation grammatically appropriate to the target language? Write the line numbers for any parts of the passage that you would like help with.

    _____

    _____

    _____

    _____

3. Does your translation indicate any linguistic biases? In order to look for bias in your work, examine your source language competence with regard to the passage. Examine your target language competence with regard to the passage. Is your translation grammatically appropriate to the target language? Do you have any biases regarding either of your languages or the subject matter? If your translation follows English word order instead of the word order of the target language that may represent a bias in favor of English or it may represent lack of competence in the target language, either of which can negatively affect the translation.

_____

_____

_____

_____

4. Check your translation to see if the temporal relations have been held constant in the transfer process. You can determine this by outlining the order of events in the source and target texts and comparing outlines.

_____

_____

_____

_____

5. Did you use visualization to help you establish the spatial relations in the text? If so how did that help? If not, go back and visualize in your mind's eye all the information.

Were you able to preserve the logical relations? Remember this means that the cause and effect relationships are preserved. If you have questions about how to preserve these relations, write them here.

_____

_____

_____

_____

Five-Step Follow-up

Step 1   **Observation**

Review your translation and answers to the study questions.

Step 2   **Selection**

Circle any portion of the source text whose translation you would like to improve. Were these places where you had distracting self-talk?

Step 3   **Analysis**

Describe the thought processes you used during transfer to determine relations (temporal, spatial and logical) and check the target text to see if you have dealt appropriately with any idioms, figurative terms, or general and specific terms.

_____

_____

_____

_____

Step 4   **Assessment**

Review your translations and your answers to the study questions to note how your translation is affected by the transfer process. Check whether you have made progress with the new techniques regarding the transfer process; checking your work for biases with the topic and languages involved, maintaining relations within the text, and translating idioms, figurative language and general/specific concepts. If you notice problems in any of these areas or have questions about the transfer process, write them here.

_____

_____

_____

_____

Step 5   Action

Write your plan for action based on your analysis and assessment. Review what you have discovered about your work in steps 1 through 4 and make some decisions about what steps you would like to take to improve your performance. Look at your answer to step 4 to determine where you can take action.

_____

_____

_____

_____

Progress Tracking Sheet

Use this sheet to track your progress on the exercises you have completed. After performing an exercise (one or two times), answering the study questions, and doing the follow-up, fill in the tracking sheet. Note the date that you completed the exercise and give an indication of your level of accomplishment. You can use either a quantitative or a qualitative approach to track your progress.

Exercise Number	Date	First Performance	Study Questions	Follow-up Activity	Questions and Reminders	Date	Second Performance
Exercise 3.1 Quantitative Qualitative							
Exercise 3.2 Quantitative Qualitative							
Exercise 3.3 Quantitative Qualitative							
Quantitative Totals							

UNIT
4

Reformulating the Message

Introduction

Reformulation is the visible result of the analysis and transfer stages of translation. Reformulation allows the message to take form in the target language. The translated message must conform to the target language syntax, preserve the illocutionary force of the source text, and be expressed in word choices that are appropriate to the target language. This stage is when you write down or videotape the translation in the target language. This unit focuses on six factors to be aware of during the reformulation process. The factors are reformulating the text as a whole, the main idea, locations of actors and objects, concepts and relationships, illocutionary force, and words.

Reformulate the Text

Reformulate the Main Idea

From your work at the analysis stage you are aware that you need to find the main idea and understand the text as a whole before beginning the translation. The author or speaker may state the topic and intent and provide information that supports the stated topic and intent. If the author does not state the topic and intent you may need to infer the topic and intent to understand the text as a whole. At other times the speaker may state a topic and not address it. When you do know the topic and intent of the source text you are better prepared to translate effectively. A way to begin reformulating the text as a whole is to get the gist or overall idea of the entire text and translate the gist into the target language.

Reformulate the Location of Actors and Objects

Determining the location of the actors and objects helps you find the main idea. Carefully consider how you will render the location of the actors and objects in relation to each other. You can ask yourself some questions to help organize the information in your mind. Who or what is doing the acting or initiating the action? Who or what is receiving the action? What is the action? What is the reaction? Sometimes this information is explicit and easy to find in the source text and sometimes it is not. In either case a translator needs to be aware of the locations and the possible locations of actors and objects. Even though we are now ready to reformulate the message, we still need to continually analyze the message because the stages of translation are really recursive, not linear.

Reformulate Specific Concepts and Relationships

The first sentence in the transcript to Exercise 4.1 is "A little girl picks up a tray and some utensils in the cafeteria." The sentence does not reveal the location of the tray and utensils in relation to each other and to the girl. Nevertheless, the concepts must be conveyed. If you are working into a signed language, which requires you to show the relationships between the actor (the girl) and the objects (tray and utensil), then you must establish locations and physical relationships for the actors and objects. You can do this by visualizing. You practiced visualization in the previous unit.

Visualizing the location of actors and objects is necessary before assigning a mental location to each of the actors and objects. Assigning a physical location to actors is necessary in signed languages. Spoken language interpreters may not need to explicitly state the relationships between objects or actors, but it is helpful to have a mental diagram of where the important aspects of the text are located.

If you are working into ASL or another signed language, you will need to establish the girl at a specific location in your signing space and then establish where the tray and utensils are in relation to her before and after she picks them up. Based on prior experiences in a cafeteria you might assume that the girl places the utensils on a tray. Be sure to visualize before you begin your interpretation and then keep the same mental image so your interpretation will be consistent.

The location of the utensils after the girl picks them up is not specified so be aware that if your translation shows the utensils on a tray, you have made a decision based on prior experience and inference. In other words you are establishing a hypothesis that the utensils are on a tray. A hypothesis is like a guess. You are not positive that the utensils are on a tray so you may need to make a correction later on if you find that the utensils are held in her hand rather than placed on a tray. The text does not reveal the location of trays and utensils in the cafeteria or the girl's location in the cafeteria, but the translation can be rendered without these relationships being made explicit. In this instance the risk of making an error in translating and the resulting loss of meaning would be of small consequence, but it is good practice to be aware of establishing actors and objects in mental space and possibly in signing space when you are moving through a translation that is based on a hypothesis.

Reformulate Illocutionary Force

The arrangement of information at the grammatical level of the source text lets us know if the text is a statement, question, rhetorical question, or exclamation. These various types of utterances have specific functions or illocutionary force in communication. The translation must reflect the same discourse function as the source message. For example, if the source text is a question and you convey it as a statement then the function of the text is not held constant and the effect of the translation will not be the same as the effect of the source text. This means that to translate effectively you must know how to construct the appropriate syntactic arrangement in the target language in order to create an equivalent impact on the target language audience.

Reformulate at the Word Level

Bell (1991) suggests methods for making decisions about lexical aspects of translations. Before you begin the actual reformulation process, which Bell calls synthesis, you must have a clear framework in mind for the source text.

Once you have considered the overall meaning of the source message, you can begin to develop specific word selection techniques. Some source language words will have equivalent lexical items in the target language. In those instances, it will be relatively easy to select the appropriate target language word. This does not mean that you can always use a word replacement technique to translate. You must keep the intent and context of the overall message in mind while you translate. Several methods of choosing lexical equivalents are described next.

One method of choosing lexical equivalents is *borrowing*. This means taking a word directly from the source text and using it in the target text. For example, the word "computer" is used in French, even though it is an English word. The word "computer" will be recognizable in spoken French as the word "computer." This method has application if the source and target language are both spoken or both signed.

A second method of choosing lexical equivalents is *modulation.* This represents a shift in the point of view, like the difference between asking "is this seat taken?" and "is this seat free?" Another example is seen in the fact that "no vacancy" and "full" convey the same concept from opposite viewpoints. The source can convey one point of view while the translation conveys a different point of view. It is important that the change in point of view does not change the meaning.

A third method is *adaptation.* This means selecting a culturally equivalent target language response. Bell suggests that in French people say *bon apetit* before eating a meal, but in English the equivalent is silence (p. 71). Speakers of American English may say nothing or may say something like "dig in" at the beginning of a meal.

Bell explains that when a word or concept has more than one possible translation, you automatically eliminate one translation in favor of another. Suppose that the source language has only one way to express "joy" while the target language has a variety of ways to express the concept. You must select one word or phrase from the range of possible choices in the target language. The word or phrase that you select has a slightly different meaning than the ones that you reject. Bell reminds us that it is important to be aware of all of the possible choices in the target language and to know the ramifications of selecting one word over others in a translation. This is only possible when you have strong target language skills.

The reformulation process naturally includes the possibility of some loss of meaning in the target language. Some loss is inevitable in translation due to the differences in cultures and the limitations of one language to fully convey the cultural constructs of another language. Ideally, linguistic and cultural competence in the two languages you are using, along with clear reasons for the choices you make in the translation process, can minimize loss.

Reformulating the Message Exercises

EXERCISE 4.1

Buying Lunch
DIANA GORMAN

Directions

Find and watch this selection on your tape. Write a brief description of your audience in the space provided. Answer the first two study questions and then translate the passage. If you are working into a language that has a written form, write the translation in the space provided. Keep the overall story in mind as you translate. Videotape your translation if you are working into a signed language. You may use glossing as an intermediate step before you videotape your translation. While you are translating, be aware of the location of actors, objects, and events. Be aware of which approach you use to translate the lexical items. After you complete the translation, answer the remaining study questions and do the follow-up.

_____

_____

Transcript for *Buying Lunch,* by Diana Gorman

1   A little girl picks up a tray and some utensils in a cafeteria. She puts

2   some food on the tray, including some milk. She sits across from one of

3   her friends, eating her food. When she is done eating, she picks up her

4   tray and walks off.

_____

_____

_____

_____

_____

_____

Study Questions

1. Do you have a mental picture for buying lunch in the cafeteria? How does prior experience in buying and eating lunch in the cafeteria help you reformulate the message in the target language?

   _____

   _____

   _____

   _____

2. After you listen to the video selection, visualize the sequence of events in your mind. Draw a sketch that shows the relative positions of the girl, the tray, where she sits and where she leaves her tray when she is finished. Use this diagram to help you render the translation into the target language.

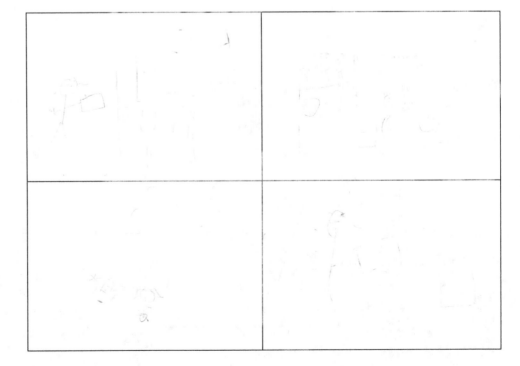

3. What method did you use in selecting lexical items to convey the message?

_____

_____

_____

_____

4. Is the syntax of the source and target language the same or different? How does knowing the syntax of the target language help you translate effectively? In the target language, what syntactic feature comes first in a statement? Does the target language utterance serve the same function as the utterance in the source language?

_____

_____

_____

_____

5. How will rearranging the locations of the actors and objects in this text affect the translation? What will happen to the message if you rearrange the order of events? Note any other problems that you found in reformulating and use these questions in your study group or ask your teacher for assistance.

_____

_____

_____

_____

Five Step Follow-up

Step 1   **Observation**

Review your translation and your answers to the study questions.

Step 2   **Selection**

Circle any source language sentences whose translations you would like to improve.

Step 3   **Analysis**

Check your translation for equivalence regarding the relative location of actors, order of events, and approaches to translation of syntactic and lexical items.

Step 4   **Assessment**

In this unit you learned about reformulating the message. Review your translations and your answers to the study questions and describe the effect of focusing on reformulating the message in the target language. For example, "My translation is equivalent, except for the last sentence. I did not know how to translate it. My reason for saying that the translation is equivalent is that I feel that the translation renders the message accurately and I made conscious decisions about the word choices I used."

_____

_____

_____

_____

Step 5   **Action**

Write a plan for action based on your analysis and assessment. In the fifth step you review what you have discovered about your work in steps 1 through 4 and make some decisions about what steps you would like to take to improve your performance.

_____

_____

EXERCISE 4.2

Ripped Pants
DIANA GORMAN

Directions

Find and listen to this selection on your tape. Write a brief description of your audience in the space provided. Answer the first two study questions. If you are working into a language that has a written form, write the translation in the space provided below the passage. Keep the overall story in mind as you translate. Videotape your translation if you are working into a signed language. You may use glossing as an intermediate step before you videotape your translation. While you are translating, be aware of the location of actors, objects, and events. Be aware of which approach you use to translate the lexical items. After you complete the translation, answer the remaining study questions and do the follow-up.

Transcript for *Ripped Pants,* by Diana Gorman

1 A little boy rips his pants climbing a fence. He then looks down and

2 notices that his pants are ripped. His mom sews the rip in his pants.

3 The little boy happily puts his pants back on.

_____

_____

Study Questions

1. To reformulate the message you need to locate the actors and objects in relation to each other. Do you have an experience of accidentally ripping and then repairing clothes? If not, can you imagine what it would be like to rip your pants while climbing over something? How does having this experience help you reformulate the message in the target language?

_____

_____

_____

_____

2. After you listen to the video selection, visualize the sequence of events in your mind. Note that the pants are ripped while he is climbing the fence, but that the text does not say if the pants are ripped while climbing up or down the fence. Draw a sketch that shows the relative positions of the boy, the fence, the mother, and the boy putting his pants back on. Use this diagram to help you render the translation into the target language.

<table>
<tr><td></td><td></td></tr>
<tr><td></td><td></td></tr>
</table>

3. What method did you use in selecting lexical items to convey the message? Consult the list of methods in this unit if you need to.

    _____

    _____

    _____

    _____

4. Are the source and target messages equivalent in illocutionary force? Why or why not?

    _____

    _____

5. What happens to the message if you rearrange the order of events?

    _____

    _____

Five-Step Follow-up

Step 1   Observation

Review your translation and your answers to the study questions.

Step 2   Selection

Select the portions of your work that are most satisfactory and select the portions that need further attention. If you are unable to translate any of the sentences, write them here in the source language. Circle source language sentences whose translations you would like to improve.

_____

_____

_____

Step 3   Analysis

Check your translation for equivalence regarding the use of relative location of actors, order of events, and approaches to translation of lexical items.

Step 4   Assessment

In this unit you learned about reformulating the message. Review your translations and your answers to the study questions to describe the effect of focusing on reformulating the message in the target language. Back up your choices with reasons.

_____

_____

_____

_____

Step 5   Action

Write a plan for action based on your analysis and assessment. In the fifth step you review what you have discovered about your work in steps 1 through 4 and make decisions about what steps you would like to take to improve your performance. Write your action plan in the space provided.

_____

_____

_____

_____

EXERCISE 4.3

A Childhood Incident

MARQUESSA BROWN

Directions

Find and watch this selection on your tape. Write a brief description of your audience below. Answer the first two study questions and then translate the passage. If you are working into a language that has a written form, write the translation in the space provided below the transcript. Keep the overall story in mind as you translate. Videotape your translation if you are working into a signed language. You may use glossing as an intermediate step before you videotape your translation. While you are translating, be aware of the schema locating actors, objects, and events. Be aware of which approach you use to translate the lexical items. After you complete the translation, answer the remaining study questions and do the follow-up.

_____

_____

Transcript for *A Childhood Incident,* by Marquessa Brown

1   Hi. I'm Marquessa. I'm going to share with you one of the most

2   special or funny events in my life. It's when I was six years old. I was

3   a very active child. Um, probably from birth, through all my life, but

4   anyway, at six I was a very active and busy kind of child. I used to

5   like to cook a lot; and play outside a lot. So that meant that I often

6   took my mom's pots and pans outside to do my cooking.

7   On one special day that I'll never forget I had taken my mom's

8   pots outside and then begun my daily cooking. And I had three pots:

9   one large one, one medium-sized one, and one very small one. The

10   large one was for my roast, which was made out of a large rock; and

11   the medium-sized one was for my vegetables, my greens which was a

12   mixture of grass and weeds; and the small one was for my potatoes,

13   which were very small pebbles. Um, I didn't have any difficulty

14   finding my grass and my weeds for my green vegetables, nor did I

15   have any difficulty finding my small pebbles for my potatoes. So I

16   quickly found both of those and got my dinner started. Well, it was a

17   little bit more difficult to find my roast, which was my larger rock.

18   There happened to be a rock that was the perfect size under the steps.

19   So, I proceeded to go to the steps and stick my head under and my

20   arms under to get this rock, which was my roast for the day.

21   I couldn't get my head out once I got it stuck! I had my roast but

22   I didn't have my head. So I moved back and forth and I tried to get

23   my head out and I couldn't! And I screamed and I yelled and finally

24   my mom came outside. She also kinda worked and helped me try to

25   get my head from under the steps. She couldn't get me from under

26   the steps either. So then my mom called a neighbor, because by this

27   time my mom was a little bit panicked. So she called the neighbor

28   and between the two of them they got me from under the steps. And

29   at that point my mother fussed at me because she—I think she was

30   angry for two reasons. First she was angry because this was just

31   another thing that I had done in my life to try her patience. And so

32   she was a little bit annoyed because I'd gotten my head stuck under

33   the steps and I couldn't get out, she couldn't get me out, and she had

34   to get a neighbor to help her get me out; and then she was annoyed

35   because I had her good pots and pans outside with rocks in them.

36   And I think what I forgot to share was I had also made my gravy,

37   which was a combination of dirt and water, meaning mud. So I had

38   this mud and these rocks, which were my potatoes, and all this gooky

39   stuff in my mother's good pots and pans. So she was furious, and so

40   that ended up being another one of those times where I was on

41   punishment and sent to my room where I always went to the window

42   and yelled out, "Hi! I'm on punishment! Guess what I did this time!"

_____

_____

_____

_____

_____

_____

_____

_____

_____

_____

_____

_____

_____

_____

_____

_____

_____

_____

Study Questions

1. Have you had an experience like getting your head stuck in stairs or for pretending to cook? If you do not have that exact experience do you have one that is similar? For example did you ever get your hand stuck in a jar or other small place? How do prior experiences help you reformulate the message in the target language?

    _____

    _____

    _____

    _____

2. After you listen to the video selection, visualize the sequence of events in your mind. Draw a sketch that shows the relative positions of the girl, the steps, the mother, her pots and pans, and where she is when she is yelling to passersby. Use this diagram to help you render the main points of the translation into the target language. Note that the speaker does not describe the exact locations and spatial relationships of actors and objects. However, you will find it easier to translate the passage if you assign actors and objects to specific places in your mind's eye.

3. Which methods did you use for lexical reformulation? If you find you use the same method in each translation, try another method and see how it affects the translation.

_____

_____

_____

_____

4. With regard to the utterance "Hi! I'm on punishment! Guess what I did this time!" how does the illocutionary force of this part of the passage differ from the rest of the passage? Does your translation reflect this difference?

_____

_____

_____

_____

5. How will it affect the translation if you rearrange the locations of the actors and objects in this text? How will it affect the translation if you change the order of events?

_____

_____

_____

_____

Five-Step Follow-up

Step 1   Observation

Review your translation and your answers to the study questions.

Step 2   Selection

Select the portions of your work that are most satisfactory and select the portions that need further attention. Circle any portion of the source text that was difficult to translate. Circle any source language sentences whose translations you would like to improve.

_____

_____

_____

_____

Step 3   Analysis

Check your translation for equivalence regarding relative location of actors, order of events, and approaches to translation of syntactic and lexical items.

Step 4   Assessment

In this unit you focused on reformulating the message. Review your translations and your answers to the study questions and discribe the effect of focusing on reformulating the message in the target language. Back up your choices with reasons.

_____

_____

_____

_____

Step 5   Action

Develop a plan for action based on your analysis and assessment.

In the fifth step you review what you have discovered about your work in steps 1 through 4 and make some decisions about what steps you would like to take to improve your performance.

_____

_____

_____

_____

Progress Tracking Sheet

Use this sheet to track your progress with the exercises you have completed. After performing an exercise (one or two times), answering the study questions, and doing the follow-up, fill in the tracking sheet. Note the date that you completed the exercise and give an indication of your level of accomplishment. You can use either a quantitative or a qualitative approach to track your progress.

Exercise Number	Date	First Performance	Study Questions	Follow-up Activity	Questions and Reminders	Date	Second Performance
Exercise 4.1 Quantitative Qualitative							
Exercise 4.2 Quantitative Qualitative							
Exercise 4.3 Quantitative Qualitative							
Quantitative Totals							

UNIT
5

Priorities in Translation

Introduction

Having covered the basic approaches to translation; preparation, analysis, transfer and reformulation, we can now emphasize priorities in translation. The highest priority in translation is rendering a message in the target language that is equivalent to the source language message. After considering the overall meaning, grammatical form, and lexical issues, you must also consider how all these components fit together to create equivalence. Strategies for achieving equivalence between source and target messages are the focus of this unit. The discussion of equivalence is separated from the discussion of testing the translation project as a whole. Testing the translation is discussed in Unit 6.

The word "equivalent" means "a very close similarity in meaning as opposed to similarity in form." (Nida & Tabor, 1982, p. 200). Snell-Hornby (1995) reports that Beaugrande says equivalence is "a valid representation of the original in the communicative act. (Beaugrande, 1978, p. 14; cited in Snell-Hornby, 1995, p. 21). Snell-Hornby concludes that in striving to achieve equivalence, translators must (1) take into account the cultural aspects of both the source and target languages, (2) admit that there are "blurred edges" between meanings in various languages, and (3) account for the "web of relationships" that exist between individual words and the larger context in which they are situated and which accounts for culture, text, and situation (p. 35). From these brief descriptions of equivalence, we can see that equivalence is not a black and white issue. Understanding equivalence requires study, linguistic maturity, and some tolerance for ambiguity.

In the past 25 years, in the field of translation studies there has been much discussion of the notion of equivalence and what it really means. Various authors have attempted to define equivalence or refute other authors' definitions of equivalence. The long-standing controversy over its definition highlights the difficulty in understanding what equivalence means. Snell-Hornby (1995) says that one approach to defining equivalence is to say that equivalence is selecting the "optimal equivalent" from a set of "potential equivalents." This approach is problematic because it uses the word equivalent in its solution. Snell-Hornby says this idea is on shaky ground because it assumes a certain amount of *symmetry* between languages. Symmetry in this case means an exact correspondence between the meanings of words in different languages. Snell-Hornby goes on to illustrate the fact that the word "equivalence" and its German "counterpart" *aquivalenz* do not mean exactly the same thing, even though the two words look and sound similar. The goal is to create a translation that preserves as much of the meaning and impact while being culturally relevant in the target language. The translator must have enough competence in the source and target language and in translation (analysis, transfer, and reformulation) to be able to determine if the source and target text are equivalent in meaning.

Priorities in Translation

According to Nida and Tabor, each language has its own genius; anything that can be said in one language can be said in another. (1992, p. 4). Nida and Tabor originally wrote guidelines for Bible translation, but their guidelines serve a broader purpose. Many schools of translation refer to these authors for information on translation theory. Nida and Tabor suggest that the following three priorities for achieving equivalence in translating will improve your translations. You have been introduced to these topics in earlier units and their presentation here serves to review and emphasize their importance.

Contextual Consistency

The first priority in achieving equivalence in translation is contextual consistency. This means that the translator must be aware of the context that surrounds the source language message and that the form of the target language message must reflect the context in which it is delivered. This priority reflects the fact that translations demonstrate the importance of linguistic forms that are appropriate to the target language. In the introduction we saw that some languages have one word to express a concept while others have many words to express the same concept. In translation, meaning must be preserved, rather than form. At the same time the form must be appropriate to the target language.

Contextual consistency means that words cover areas of meaning and are not discrete points of isolated meaning. Choosing the "correct" word in the target language will depend on the word's context in the source text and the translator's understanding of the source text. For example, some words are only used in certain contexts. The translator must be aware of context in both the source and the target language when selecting ways to express the concepts in the target language.

Dynamic Equivalence and Formal Correspondence

Dynamic Equivalence

Dynamic equivalence means the translation has the same impact on the target audience as the original text did on the original audience. Dynamic equivalence takes into account the contexts in which the source and target messages occur. Sometimes the terms "dynamic equivalence and "equivalence" are used interchangeably but the term dynamic equivalence is a broader term and generally includes making cultural adjustments to the translation so that the impact of the message is preserved. For example, Snell-Hornby (1995) cites Nida and Tabor's famous example from Bible translation studies. This example shows that the term "Lamb" in "Lamb of God" symbolizes innocence. But in the Eskimo culture the word "lamb" would not have any particular significance or impact. For Eskimo culture the appropriate phrase would be "Seal of God" because seals represent innocence in Eskimo culture. To achieve the best possible equivalence, it is important to place a higher priority on dynamic equivalence than formal correspondence in a translation.

Formal Correspondence

Nida and Tabor (1992) say that formal correspondence is the opposite of dynamic equivalence. Formal correspondence means that the features of the form of the source text have been mechanically reproduced in the target language. It is similar to a literal translation. Formal correspondence typically distorts the grammatical and stylistic patterns of the target language and thus distorts the message. Formal correspondence not only distorts the message but also causes the person who is reading the translation or receiving the interpretation to labor unduly to understand or to misunderstand (p.201). The target audience should not have to struggle to understand the message. As Nida and Tabor say, "the best translation does not sound like a translation."

Nida and Tabor (1982, p. 200) state that dynamic equivalence allows the message to be transported from the source to the target language in a way that allows the responses to either source or target to be essentially the same. They go on to say that the form of the text is changed to comply with the structural requirements of the form of the target language, but the content of the message in the target language must be faithful to the content of the message in the source text. Their explanation emphasizes the importance of preserving meaning, not form, in translation.

The priority of dynamic equivalence over formal correspondence reflects the reactions of the audience, their cultural understandings, and the context of the message. In this priority, intelligibility of the target message, especially in terms of its impact on the target audience, takes precedence over formal correspondence or a word-for-word translation. There is one inherent problem in this priority. Members of the original audience can only express the impact of the original message in words. We have already discovered that words are often only an approximation of an experience. When the message is translated into the target language, the same problem arises. The members of the target audience must use words to describe the impact of the message. If the responses of the original and target audiences are dissimilar, there might be a lack of dynamic equivalence in the translation. Since there is no absolute equivalence of word meanings between languages, we can only approximate the similarity of impact on the two audiences.

Although we cannot measure the impact of the message on either audience directly, Nida and Tabor suggest that there are other ways to consider the impact of a message. One way to determine impact may be to look at the functions of the source and target texts and consider the responses of the audience. There may be differences in aural and written information. For example, if the message is a statement, the audience obtains information. If the message is in the form of a question, the audience ponders the question. Some other functions of a message include imperative function (commands), persuasion, or to evoke emotion. So another way to look at impact is to see how the message functions in the context and on the target audience.

Audience Needs

The third priority reflects factors such as age, sex, education, and background experience of the audience. (Nida & Tabor, 1992, p. 14). Nida and Tabor suggest that the linguistic forms that the audience can understand and accept must take precedence over forms that may have greater prestige, such as more formal or technical language. Ideally, the message will "fit" the linguistic needs of the intended audience. Although this is the ideal, the translator may not be able to achieve this if the linguistic needs of the audience are unknown. Throughout this book you have been asked to describe your intended audience. As a professional translator, you may know the intended audience, but may not know the actual audience. While developing translation skill, it is useful to have a specific audience in mind even though we do not know who will eventually use the translation. Another factor to consider is that audiences are rarely homogenous and often the translator must render a translation that can suit the most people.

Fitting the translation or interpretation to the needs of the audience is a complex and important issue. Interpreters have the benefit of being able to interact with the audience because interpretation occurs in real time, while translators do not have the benefit of this interaction. How much "adjustment" the translator or interpreter must make in order to have the message understood by the audience is widely debated in both fields. My position is that both translators and interpreters should consider the needs of the audience as much as possible. This is an ideal because audiences are rarely homogeneous in terms of linguistic needs. Furthermore, the translator or interpreter may not know the linguistic needs of the actual audience. It is also possible that the intent of the source text creator could be in conflict with the target audience's linguistic needs. For example the creator of the source text may intend to be vague or to confuse. In that instance the needs of the target language audience may not be met by the translation.

The exercises in this workbook do not describe the linguistic needs of the audiences. You can create a description of a hypothetical audience for each exercise and you can create alternate translations for audiences that have different linguistic needs. Additional factors regarding audience needs are addressed in the Introduction to Translating from English.

Nida and Tabor propose that the three priorities of contextual consistency, dynamic equivalence and formal correspondence, and audience needs must be considered in the translation process. Other authors have different approaches to describing priorities in translation.

In summary, translations must preserve the meaning of the source message. Nida and Tabor emphasize the underlying priority of meaning over form and state, " radical departures from formal structure are not only legitimate but may even be highly desirable" (p. 13). These authors also write that the "best translation does not sound like a translation" and the aim is to "reproduce the message" (p. 12). At the same time, the authors emphasize that the translation must be *intelligible*. This intelligibility includes (1) understandable and appropriate word selection, (2) grammatically correct sentence structure, and (3) the total impact of the message on the one who receives it. These three criteria form the basis for the exercises in this unit. Keep the priorities described above in mind as you do the exercises in this unit. When these criteria are consistently met equivalence is more likely to be achieved.

Translation Priority Exercises

EXERCISE 5.1

The Car Wash
DIANA GORMAN

Directions

Find and watch this selection on your tape. Describe the intended audience in the space provided. If you are working into a language that has a written form, write the translation in the space provided below the transcript. If you are working into a signed language, videotape your translation. You may use glossing as an intermediate step in translating from printed English to a signed language Keep the overall passage in mind as you translate. Be aware of the priorities suggested by Nida and Tabor. After you complete the translation, answer the study questions and do the follow-up.

_____

_____

Transcript for *The Car Wash,* by Diana Gorman

1   A man drives his car up to a car wash. As his car goes through the car

2   wash, soap surrounds the car. When he drives his car out of the car

3   wash, water cascades down the car. When the car is dry, he drives off

4   and it is sparkling clean.

_____

_____

_____

_____

_____

_____

Study Questions

1. Does your translation meet the criteria of dynamic equivalence? How do you know?

_____

_____

_____

_____

2. Examine your translation for understandable and appropriate word choices. How do you determine understandability of the translated message? How do you decide if the word choices are appropriate for the target language?

_____

_____

_____

_____

3. Does any part of your translation rely on formal correspondence? If so, why?

_____

_____

_____

_____

4. Does your translation indicate the same punctuation marks and discourse markers that convey the intent of the source text? Are questions rendered as questions? Are statements rendered as statements? If you are working into a signed language how do you show the beginning and end of sentences?

_____

_____

_____

_____

5. Examine the translation of the following adjectives from the text to see if the impact of the translation is the same as when you first heard the word or read the word.

cascades

sparkling

_____

_____

_____

_____

Five-Step Follow-up

Be sure that your translation and the answers to the study questions are complete before starting the follow-up.

Step 1   Observation

Review your translation and your answers to the study questions.

Step 2   Selection

Refer to the transcript and circle any portions of it that you were not able to translate or that you have questions about. Write the line numbers in the space provided. Refer to your answers to the study questions and circle the number of any study question that you need assistance with. Write the numbers of the study questions in the space provided.

_____

_____

_____

_____

Step 3   Analysis

Remember that the focus is on the equivalence of the message between source and target languages. The translation exercise allows you to create a product. The study questions allow you to examine your product by highlighting the various aspects of equivalence and help determine whether you have established equivalence and intelligibility. The follow-up allows you to develop insight into processes you used to create the product.

Analyze your translation for equivalence. Refer to the sentences you circled in step 2 of the follow-up. Give yourself a score of 0–5 for each sentence, with 0 indicating the absence of equivalence and 5 indicating strong equivalence. Scoring is arbitrary but can be a helpful device. Alternatively, you can note if each sentence is "equivalent," "not equivalent," or "I don't know if it is equivalent." For each sentence that is not equivalent, state why it is not equivalent. For example, the word order is inappropriate, some word choices are misleading, or perhaps you did not know how to express a concept in the target language.

_____

_____

_____

_____

Step 4   Assessment

This step allows you to assess your work objectively. Examine your answers to step 3 of the follow-up. Write down the possible underlying causes for lack of equivalence in the space provided. If you circled some portions of the transcript because you were not able to provide a translation, what are the underlying reasons that you were unable to establish equivalence? What are the probable effects of lack of equivalence on the target language audience?

_____

_____

_____

_____

Step 5   **Action**

Develop a plan for action based on your analysis and assessment. Review what you have discovered about your work in steps 1 through 4 and make some decisions about what steps to take to improve your performance. Write your plan of action for improvement in the space provided.

_____

_____

_____

_____

EXERCISE 5.2

Sharpening a Pencil

DIANA GORMAN

Directions

Find and watch this selection on your tape. Describe the intended audience in the space provided. If you are working into a language that has a written form, write the translation in the space below the source text. If you are working into a signed language, videotape your translation. You may use glossing as an intermediate step in going from printed English to a signed language. Keep the overall story in mind as you translate. Focus on the priorities for translation and criteria for intelligibility suggested by Nida and Tabor. After you complete the translation, answer the study questions and do the follow-up.

_____

_____

Transcript for *Sharpening a Pencil,* by Diana Gorman

1   As a girl is writing her letter, her pencil breaks. She takes the broken

2   pencil up to a pencil sharpener. She sharpens her pencil. The girl

3   resumes writing her letter.

_____

_____

_____

_____

_____

Study Questions

1. Does your translation meet the criteria of dynamic equivalence? How do you know?

2. Examine your translation for understandable and appropriate word choices. How do you determine understandability of the translated message? How do you decide if the word choices are appropriate for the target language?

_____

_____

_____

_____

3. Does any part of your translation rely on formal correspondence? If so, why?

    _____

    _____

    _____

    _____

4. Does your translation indicate the same punctuation marks and discourse markers that convey the intent of the source text? If you are working into a signed language how do you show the beginning and end of sentences? How do you show questions? How do you show negation?

    _____

    _____

    _____

    _____

5. Examine the following verbs from the text to see if the impact of the translation is the same as when you first heard or read the word:

    sharpens

    resumes

    _____

    _____

    _____

    _____

Five-Step Follow-up

Be sure that your translation and the answers to the study questions are complete before starting the follow-up.

Step 1   Observation

Review your translation and your answers to the study questions.

Step 2   Selection

Refer to the transcript and circle any portions of it that you were not able to translate or that you have questions about. Write the line numbers in the space provided.

Refer to your answers to the study questions and circle the number of any study question that you need assistance with. Write the numbers of the questions in the space provided.

_____

_____

_____

_____

Step 3   Analysis

Remember that the focus is on the equivalence of the message between source and target languages. The translation exercise allows you to create a product. The study questions allow you to examine your product by highlighting the various aspects of equivalence and help determine whether you have established equivalence and intelligibility. The follow-up allows you to develop insight into processes you used to create the product.

Analyze your translation for equivalence. Refer to the sentences you circled in step 2 of the follow-up. Give yourself a score of 0–5 for each sentence, with 0 indicating the absence of equivalence and 5 indicating strong equivalence. Scoring is arbitrary but can be a helpful device in determining wheter you have established equivalence. Alternatively, you can note if each sentence is "equivalent," "not equivalent," or "I don't know if it is equivalent." For each sentence that is not equivalent, state why it is not equivalent. For example, the word order is inappropriate, some word choices are misleading, or perhaps you did not know how to express a concept in the target language.

_____

_____

_____

_____

Step 4   Assessment

This step allows you to assess your work objectively. Examine your answers to step 3 of the follow-up. Write down the possible underlying causes for lack of equivalence in the space provided. If you circled some portions of the transcript because you were not able to provide a translation, what are the underlying reasons that you were unable to establish equivalence? What is the effect of lack of equivalence on the target language audience?

_____

_____

_____

_____

Step 5   Action

Develop a plan for action based on your analysis and assessment. Review what you have discovered about your work in steps 1 through 4 and make some decisions about what steps you would like to take to improve your performance. Write your plan of action for improvement in the space provided.

_____

_____

_____

_____

EXERCISE 5.3

Kelsey, Melissa, Stephanie

The Gift

BOBBI JORDAN

Directions

Find and watch this selection on your tape. Describe the intended audience in the space provided. Refer to the printed transcript and render the translation in the space below the source text. If you are working into a language that has a written form, write the translation below the source text in the space provided. If you are working into a signed language, videotape your translation. You may use glossing as an intermediate step in going from printed English to a signed language. Keep the overall story in mind as you translate. As you translate, be aware of the priorities for translation suggested by Nida and Tabor. After you complete the translation, answer the study questions and do the follow-up.

_____

_____

Note: *The Gift* appeared in an earlier volume of the *Effective Interpreting Series, Cognitive Processing Skills in English.* This selection appeared in the unit on comprehension. If you worked with this text before, it is "warm" or familiar material to you. Familiarity with the text may make it easier for you to translate the information.

Transcript for *The Gift,* by Bobbi Jordan

Melissa

1   Hi. My name is Bobbi Jordan, and I'd like to tell you a story that

2   changed my life. When I first came to California I had a very good

3   friend who lived in a tiny community and she's the person who told

4   me this story, so I have it second-hand. At that time, a young priest

5   came to that community; and we're going to call him by the name of

6   John. It was a small community and they were thrilled to have a

7   young priest with new ideas who was an exciting person and brought

8   that Catholic church to life.

9   The community was so happy about this that they got together

10   and they redid the parish hall. The men who were carpenters put new

11   wood into the house, and the plumbers redid the plumbing, and one

12   man was a tile person so the bathroom was tiled in a beautiful sage

13   green tile, and the community went out of its way to make this a

14   wonderful living place for this young priest.

15   Well, my friend, who was married with three young children and

16   had a husband who had a small business, didn't have a lot of money.

17   She didn't work. And so she had to scrimp and to save from her

18   grocery money and from other money coming in to give her present

19   to the priest for the rectory. She bought towels for the bathroom. She

20   went shopping until she found exactly the right shade of green, and

21   they were very expensive towels and she was so proud of her gift; and

22   wrapped it carefully and took it to him. And said, "Here, Father, this

23   is my gift for the rectory." He smiled, he was very pleased, and he

24   knew that she was giving him the gift out of love.

25   About a year later, my friend went to Annie's house. Annie was a

26   woman who had just lost her son, and so all the women in the

27   community were taking casseroles and giving comfort because the son

28   was a young boy and Annie was quite depressed. While my friend

29   was there she went into Annie's bathroom; and hanging in the

30   bathroom were the very towels that she had bought for the priest! She

31   looked at them and couldn't believe her eyes—she knew they weren't

32   Annie's. Annie didn't have any money, and besides, Annie's bathroom

33   was salmon—who would have picked green towels? She went back

34   out and she didn't say a word to Annie.

35   Instead, the next day she went to the rectory, knocked on the

36   door, had a small conversation with Father, and then said, "I don't

37   understand. I was over at Annie's yesterday, and I saw the towels that

38   I gave you hanging in her bathroom." Father said, "Yes, that's right."

39   My friend said, "But I worked hard for those—and I saved my money

40   and I scrimped and I saved so I could give you this gift!" Father

41   looked her in the eye and said, "But, my dear, Annie needed them."

42   And that's when I had that wonderful recognition that only comes

43   once in a lifetime. That there was a great lesson to be learned here.

44   And the lesson is this: When you give a gift, it is gone. You give it,

45   you give it to the person that you love, and then you let go of it. You

46   let it be. If that person, be it your Aunt Tillie, your best friend, wants

47   to take that gift and give it away the very next day, that's just fine—

48   because you have given, not the object, but your love. That was an

49   important lesson for me to learn that day, and that's my story.

_____

_____

_____

_____

_____

_____

_____

_____

_____

_____

_____

_____

_____

_____

_____

_____

_____

_____

_____

_____

_____

Study Questions

1. Does your translation meet the criteria of dynamic equivalence? How do you know?

   _____

   _____

2. Examine your translation for understandable and appropriate word choices. How do you determine understandability of the translated message? How do you decide if the word choices are appropriate for the target language?

   _____

   _____

_____

_____

3. Does any part of your translation rely on formal correspondence? If so, why?

_____

_____

4. Does your translation indicate the effect conveyed by the speaker? Does your translation accurately convey that different people "spoke" in the course of the passage?

_____

_____

_____

_____

5. Examine the impact of the translation and compare it to that of the source text. Do this by reading or watching your translation and comparing it to the original text. Does your work preserve any repetitions and hesitations? Why or why not?

_____

_____

_____

_____

Five-Step Follow-up

Be sure that your translation and the answers to the study questions are complete before starting the follow-up.

Step 1   Observation

Review your translation and your answers to the study questions.

Step 2   Selection

Circle any portions of the transcript that you were not able to translate or that you have questions about. Write the line numbers in the space provided.

Refer to your answers to the Study Questions and circle the number of any study question that you need assistance with. Write the numbers of the study questions in the space provided.

_____

_____

_____

_____

Step 3   Analysis

Analyze your translation for equivalence. Refer to the sentences you circled in step 2 of the follow-up. Give yourself a score of 0–5 for each sentence, with 0 indicating the absence of equivalence and 5 indicating strong equivalence. Scoring is arbitrary but can be a helpful device in determining whether you have established equivalence. Alternatively, you can note if each sentence is "equivalent," "not equivalent," or "I don't know if it is equivalent." For each sentence that is not equivalent, state why it is not equivalent. For example, the word order is inappropriate, some word choices are misleading, or perhaps you did not know how to express a concept in the target language.

_____

_____

_____

_____

Step 4   Assessment

This step allows you to assess your work objectively. Examine your answers to step 3 of the follow-up. Write down the possible underlying causes for lack of equivalence in the space provided. If you circled some portions of the transcript because you were not able to provide a translation, what are the underlying reasons that you were unable to establish equivalence? What is the effect of lack of equivalence on the target language audience?

_____

_____

_____

_____

Step 5   Action

Review what you discovered about your work in steps 1 through 4 and write the steps to improve your performance.

_____

_____

_____

_____

Progress Tracking Sheet

Use this sheet to track your progress with the exercises you have completed. After performing an exercise (one or two times), answering the study questions, and doing the follow-up, fill in the tracking sheet. Note the date that you completed the exercise and give an indication of your level of accomplishment. You can use either a quantitative or a qualitative approach to track your progress.

Exercise Number	Date	First Performance	Study Questions	Follow-up Activity	Questions and Reminders	Date	Second Performance
Exercise 5.1 Quantitative							
Qualitative							
Exercise 5.2 Quantitative							
Qualitative							
Exercise 5.3 Quantitative							
Qualitative							
Quantitative Totals							

UNIT
6

Testing the Translation

Introduction

After translating the text, the next step is testing the translation. Just as there are many theories of translation, there are many approaches to testing translations. Nida and Tabor's and Larson's approaches to testing a translating are summarized in this unit. These approaches share a common concern for evaluating the product or observable part of the translation, but not the process. In keeping with the goals of this book, however, we will also examine the processes used in translation in order to understand the source of translation errors and their impact with the goal of improved accuracy and fidelity in translation.

Why Test a Translation?

Larson (1984) asks four main questions; Why test a translation? Who tests the translation? How to test the translation? How to use the results of testing? Larson says it is important to test a translation to know whether a translation that is faithful to the source text message and that is natural sounding in the target language has been achieved. According to Larson the three elements to check when testing a translation are (1) accuracy, (2) clarity, and (3) naturalness.

Accuracy

Larson says that an accurate translation conveys all of the information that is justified by the source text. She explains that sometimes the translator struggles to reformulate the message and may include information that is not justified or warranted by the source text. In such cases, the additional information must be removed from the translation. Other authors such as Nida and Tabor (1992) state that implicit information must be made explicit in some cases, depending on the nature of the culture and language associated with the target text. These authors may seem to be contradicting each other but they are not really. They are each saying that at all costs the translation must convey the intended message without extraneous information.

Clarity

By clarity Larson means that the translation must be understandable to the people who are depending on it for information. She explains that it is possible for a translation to be accurate without being clear. An unclear translation generally contains ambiguity. Ambiguity is present when a phrase or sentence could have more than one meaning in a specific context. For example, an accurate but unclear translation of how to plant bulbs could contain correct information but present it in a confusing manner so that the target language audience is not sure of the intended meaning.

Naturalness

Larson explains that a translation can be accurate and clear and still not be natural. A natural translation is idiomatic and uses the grammatical forms ordinarily used in the target language. She suggests the following questions in relation to testing for naturalness. Does the translation "flow" easily? Does it "sound right" to speakers of the language or does it sound "foreign?" Ideally the translation does not sound like a translation, instead it sounds like a text originally created in that language.

Who Tests the Translation and When?

Larson suggests that the translator should check the translation section by section as it is developed. For example, it is best to check each paragraph as you create it rather than wait until you have completed the entire translation, especially if it is a lengthy one. Checking sections as you go along may reveal problems you can correct early in the translation process. Even if you check your work as you go along, it is a good idea to check the entire translation again after it is completed.

Once the entire translation is competed is an ideal time for a second person to review the translation. Larson suggests that this person be unfamiliar with the source language, as then the person can check for naturalness and clarity, but not accuracy. In order to check for accuracy, the tester must be familiar with both languages. At some point it is best to have a tester who can test for accuracy. Sometimes the translator must be responsible for testing for accuracy and sometimes a second translator can test for accuracy.

How Do You Test the Translation?

Larson suggests five ways to test a translation. There is some overlap between these approaches. Keep in mind that these tests examine the product of the translation, not the process used to create the translation.

Comparison with the Source Language

The first type of translation test that Larson describes is a test of the product by comparing the translation with the source language. Comparisons should be made periodically during the translation process. The purpose of comparison is to check the equivalence of the content between source and target texts. The comparison can be made by the translator or by a second translator. Nida and Tabor (1982) say that of all the possible criteria you can use to test the translation, dynamic equivalence is the most important. This means that the content of the source language message is well preserved and conveyed and has approximately the same impact as the target language.

Back Translation

The second way to test a translation according to Larson (1987) is by using back translation. Someone other than the translator should do the back translation. This means that the target text is translated back into the source language by a person who is unfamiliar with the source message. This type of test focuses on the product. The back translation is usually done in a literal rather than idiomatic fashion. Back translation indicates whether the translation has faithfully preserved the content of the source text.

Comprehension

The third type of translation test that Larson proposes is a comprehension test. This is a test of the product and is not performed by the translator, but rather is performed by a person who is a speaker of the target language. The purpose is to see if speakers of the target language understand the translation correctly. This test helps the translator determine whether the translation accurately communicates the message to the intended audience. The tester retells the content of the translation and answers questions about the content. The drawback of this approach is that the retelling depends on the tester's level of comprehension and ability to retell accurately.

Naturalness

Larson says that one of the reviewers who read the translation and commented on it should perform the naturalness test. A test of naturalness asks if the translation sounds as if it were a text originally created in the target language. Does it use the language constructions that users of the target language would use in this context? The reviewer will examine the translation for natural target language use and appropriate style. Reviewers can comment on the accuracy of the translation only if they have strong competence in the source language. The reviewer who comments on naturalness does not usually comment on accuracy and clarity because the test of naturalness does not include testing equivalence.

Readability

Readability testing applies only to languages that are written. This type of test involves having the translation read out loud by another person. Larson explains that if the reader stumbles or looks puzzled at a particular spot in the translation, then the translator should reexamine that portion of the translation for appropriate language use.

Overall Length

Nida and Tabor (1982) stress that it is usual for a written translation to be slightly longer than the original written text. They say that the overall increase in length is due to the need to state everything that was included in the original and to make explicit some things that may be implicit in the original text. We do not yet have enough data to know if this generalization applies to signed language translations.

Other key factors to watch for in the translation are that the overall organization of the target text retains the same main points and details in the same order whenever possible. The impact of the total message should not be distorted by the translation. The translator should not explicitly interject his or her own opinions into the translation; however, translators do occasionally add notes to explain or clarify a point.

How Do You Use the Results of Testing?

Gile (1994) emphasizes that there are some pitfalls in evaluating a translation solely on the basis of the product, especially for translation students. One problem with focusing on the product is that the student may not understand the real reason for the error, but think they do. Students may know that the translation is faulty in some aspect but not know why or how to correct it.

I strongly suggest that a combined approach of examining both product and process in testing the translation is most effective. You should look at the product of your translation and also work to examine the processes you used. Reread the *Introduction to Translating from English* to refresh your understanding of the difference between process and product.

Gile suggests that while you are in translator training you are really studying the methods of translation rather than "finished products" (1994, p. 108). Gile says that the problems that surface in your translations are symptoms of weaknesses in specific parts of translation methodology. The main value in looking for the errors in methods is that making changes at the method level can improve product and provide a deeper understanding of translation processes.

Awareness of where in the process errors can occur can lead to improved translations in a systematic fashion. Gile says that if grammatical errors are apparent, this usually means that you did not "perform an acceptability test properly" (p. 110). An illogical translation usually means that during the comprehension phase you did not perform hypothesis testing, or did not perform it completely. This emphasizes the fact that you must comprehend the message before you can translate it. You must determine how the major points of the text relate to each other before translating.

Recognizing ways to improve your methods makes testing translations a critical skill for students of translation.

Taxonomy of Errors

Not all errors are equally serious. It is important to sort errors by level of seriousness. Less serious errors will not have as great an impact on the message as more serious errors. If you are able to sort errors by their level of seriousness you can reduce the overall anxiety about making errors and not create unnecessary negative self-talk.

Diana Gorman (1989) has proposed the following taxonomy, or classification system, as a way to categorize errors.

Not serious—

an error that does not skew the message; usually reformulation

Somewhat serious—

an error that does not skew the message: omission of detail or production error

Quite serious—

total skew of the message due to following English syntax instead of target languale syntax

Very serious—

total skew of the message due to comprehension problems

Determing the Seriousness of Errors

If an error occurs early in the translation process, at the analysis stage for example, it is likely that there will be more serious errors in the remaining stages of the process. If you do not correctly understand the message you will not be able to transfer or reformulate it. If you can understand the message but can not transfer it, you will have difficulty reformulating it. By considering the location of the error in the translation process it becomes clear that the earlier in the process that the error occurs, the more serious the effect of the error. For example if the error occurs at the comprehension stage, the error will undoubtedly be classified as very serious. If the error occurs at later stages in the translation process it is likely to be categorized as less serious.

In the exercises in this unit you create and test a translation. In addition to the exercises in this unit, you can use the testing procedure on any other translation you have completed.

Translation Testing Exercises

EXERCISE 6.1
_____

Autobiography
ARLENE FONG CRAIG
_____

Directions

Find and watch this selection on your tape to become familiar with the speaker and the content. Write a description of your audience in the space provided. If you are working into a language that has a written form, write the translation in the space below the source text. If you are working into a signed language, videotape your translation. You may use glossing as an intermediate step in preparing your videotaped translation. Keep the overall text in mind as you translate. After you complete the translations, answer the study questions and do the follow-up. You will need a blue and a red pen or pencil for this exercise.

_____

_____

Transcript for *Autobiography,* by Arlene Fong Craig

1 Good morning. My name is Arlene Fong Craig. I consider myself a

2 bilingual individual, bicultural, and a native Philadelphian. The

3 bicultural part of my heritage came to the United States across their

4 respective oceans. My great-grandfather in the early 1880s from

5 Southern China to California, where he ran a laundry in what was left

6 of the mining fields. And he eventually became a lumberjack in

7   Seattle before Washington became a state. My great-grandmom, at the

8   same time, was coming over from England-we're not quite sure from

9   which city or from which town—but she settled in Philadelphia and

10 became a teacher and a Sunday school teacher. And eventually, these

11 two individuals met in Philadelphia, and they became my great-

12 grandparents. Many of you may be saying, "Okay, cut to the chase;

13 what do your ancestors have to do with this?" But what's past is

14 prologue. And so, this really is an important part of who I am.

15 Right now, I am working on developing university/community

16 partnerships-collaborative working relationships between universities

17 and their surrounding communities. And this is part of my work, as a

18 person who develops and implements education and outreach

19 programs. So the story is still developing on who I am, and my

20 present is my prologue for the future.

_____

_____

_____

_____

_____

_____

_____

_____

_____

_____

Study Questions

1. How can you conduct a test of comprehension on the translation?

   _____

   _____

   _____

   _____

2. Circle in blue any parts of the transcript that you had difficulty translating. Circle in red any parts of the transcript whose translation is not equivalent.

3. Examine the translation process to improve the translation product. Refer to the parts of the transcript that you circled in study question 2 and in the areas where your translation is not equivalent. Write the line numbers of the source message in the space provided and indicate if the errors are very serious, quite serious, somewhat serious, or not serious.

   _____

   _____

   _____

   _____

4. For errors marked "very serious," at what stage in the translation process did the difficulty occur?

   _____

   _____

5. Select one paragraph of your translation and back translate it into written English. Remember that the back translation should be a literal translation. Describe what happens to the meaning when you back translate the passage.

_____

_____

_____

_____

_____

_____

_____

Five-Step Follow-up

Both the translation and the testing of the translation must be completed before you do the follow-up.

Step 1   Observation

Review your translation and your answers to the study questions.

Step 2   Selection

Select the part of the testing process you would most like to improve upon and select a portion of your translation that contained at least one error. Indicate your selection by circling the corresponding portion of the source text and write the line numbers in the space provided.

_____

_____

_____

_____

Step 3   Analysis

Analyze the error you selected in Step 2 and write down the probable cause for the error.

_____

_____

_____

_____

Step 4   Assessment

Once you have decided on a probable cause for the error you selected in step 2 describe the impact of the error on the translation. Was it a serious or not serious error? Did it affect information that came after it?

_____

_____

_____

_____

Step 5   Action

Write your plan of action to improve your performance based on what you have discovered about your work in steps 1 through 4.

_____

_____

_____

_____

EXERCISE 6.2

Kickboxing
OVERTON CAVANAUGH

Directions

Find and watch this selection on your tape to become familiar with the speaker and the content. Write a description of your audience in the space provided. If you are working into a language that has a written form, write the translation in the space below the source text. If you are working into a signed language, videotape your translation. You may use glossing as an intermediate step in preparing your videotaped translation. Keep the overall text in mind as you translate. After you complete the translations, answer the study questions and do the follow-up. You will need a blue and a red pen or pencil for this exercise.

_____

_____

Transcript for *Kickboxing,* by Overton Cavanaugh

1   Hi my name is Overton Cavanaugh and I'm-I'm a kickboxing

2   instructor. I have some guys that I-that I train, uh, uh, every Saturday

3   and Sunday morning. We go running in Rock Creek Park. OK. The

4   first thing we do, we go-we go running six to seven-seven miles in the

5   woods. We go down, up…uh, I mean, y'know, uh, horse trails,

6   whatever. It's a very, very rugged-rugged style of, uh, running. We,

7   uh, pick our paces up, we slow our paces-paces down and we also

8   sprint hills. OK, after we do that then we-then we start doing sit-ups.

9   OK. We have, uh, different forms of uh, uh, sit-ups. We, uh, work the

10   uh, middle, the lower and the obliques, which is the, uh, side. OK.

11   From there we work with logs. We-we uh, have logs on pulleys. And

12   what we do with these pulleys, we attach the legs-legs to the, uh,

13 rope that pulls the pulley. And they would have to learn to uh, to uh,

14 do front kicks, side kicks and round kicks. And all this is done with

15 the, uh, pulley. Also, after doing the pulley, we uh, I-I teach them

16 how to-how to uh, how to torque their body, use lock shots. And

17 that's also done with pulling a log. With a-a rope. And they have to

18 learn to keep their elbows close to their body, step, tur-turning their

19 bodies and throwin' shots. And this is-and this is for-for cobra shots.

_____

_____

_____

_____

_____

_____

_____

_____

_____

_____

_____

_____

Study Questions

1. While you were formulating your translation, did you ask yourself if the translation was faithful and acceptable? If not, compare your translation to the source language with these questions in mind. If you have any revisions to your translation, write them in the space provided or videotape your corrections if you are working into a signed language.

----

2. Circle in blue any parts of the transcript that you had difficulty translating. Circle in red any parts of the transcript whose translation is not equivalent.

3. Examine the translation process to improve the translation product. Refer to the parts of the transcript that you circled in study question 2 and in the areas where your translation is not equivalent. Write the line numbers of the source message in the space provided and indicate if each error is very serious, quite serious, somewhat serious, or not serious.

    _____

    _____

    _____

4. For errors marked "very serious," at what stage in the translation process did the difficulty occur?

    _____

    _____

5. Select one paragraph of your translation and back translate it into written English. Remember that the back translation should be a literal translation. Describe what happens to the meaning when you back translate the passage.

    _____

    _____

    _____

    _____

    _____

    _____

_____

_____

_____

_____

Five-Step Follow-up

Both the translation and the testing of the translation must be completed before you do the follow-up.

Step 1   Observation

Review your translation and your answers to the study questions.

Step 2   Selection

Select the part of the testing process you would most like to improve upon and select a portion of your translation that contained at least one error. Indicate your selection by circling the corresponding portion of the source text and write the line numbers in the space provided.

_____

_____

_____

_____

Step 3   Analysis

Analyze the error you selected in step 2 and write down the probable cause for the error.

_____

_____

_____

_____

Step 4   Assessment

Once you have decided on a probable cause for the error you selected in step 2, describe the impact of the error on the translation. Was it a serious or not serious error? Did it affect information that came after it?

_____

_____

_____

_____

Step 5   Action

Write your plan of action to improve your performance based on what you have discovered about your work in steps 1 through 4.

_____

_____

_____

_____

EXERCISE 6.3

Newspaper Layout
AMBER LEWNES

Directions

Find and watch this selection on your tape to become familiar with the speaker and the content. Write a description of your audience in the space provided. If you are working into a language that has a written form, write the translation in the space below the source text. If you are working into a signed language, videotape your translation. You may use glossing as an intermediate step in preparing your videotaped translation. Keep the overall text in mind as you translate. After you complete the translations, answer the study questions and do the follow-up. You will need a blue and a red pen or pencil for this exercise.

Transcript for *Newspaper Layout,* by Amber Lewnes

1   My name is Amber Lewnes and I'm gonna teach you how to make a

2   newspaper. The first thing you do is get layout pages. This is a mini-

3   model of what the paper will actually look like. First you figure out

4   how much advertising space will be going into the paper for that

5   issue. Each staff writer goes around to local businesses and asks if

6   they would like to advertise and figures out how much space they

7   want advertised in the paper. Then the space is drawn up and saved

8   for each advertiser.

9   Once that is done, stories are assigned to each staff writer and the

10   editor draws out how big the stories will be onto the pages as they fit

11   according to the ad- the advertising. So pretty much everything is

12   based around the advertising. Then the spaces for the photographs

13   are made and these spaces are then- the sizes are told to the

14   photographers, who will then make a photo to fit the space.

15   Once all the stories have been assigned and the pages have been

16   drawn out, the writers go to work and research their topics. When

17   they're done they turn in a rough copy to the editor, who then reads

18   it over and edits and makes any changes that they see fit or sees if

19   there's any inaccuracies in the story. Once that is done, the writer

20   writes it up on the computer and puts it into a program called

21   Pagemaker to be printed out to eventually be pasted onto the

22   newspaper.

23   Once the story is actually in the paper the editor will go in and
24   design the story in the computer to fit the space that is allotted. Once
25   that is done, the pr- pages are printed up and they're pasted onto a
26   large sheet of paper that's the actual size of the newspaper. The spaces
27   are left for the photos, which will be added later.

28   Once photographers take their photos they bring 'em to the editor
29   and the editor cuts them and pastes them on the page. Then they take
30   tape called line tape which is a little black line and it outlines each
31   photo so that it'll look-make the picture look more spaced out and
32   separate from the story when it's actually printed. After that is done,
33   captions are written for underneath the pictures, and those are pasted
34   onto the pages as well.

35   Then, finally, the advertisers send in their ads which are then also
36   to be pasted onto each page. After that is done, these rough pages are
37   sent to the printer to be printed in mass publication, to be distributed
38   to the school, or to the city or wherever the newspaper is intended
39   for. And that's how you make a newspaper.

_____

_____

_____

_____

_____

_____

_____

_____

_____

_____

_____

_____

_____

_____

Study Questions

1. While you were formulating your translation, did you ask yourself if the translation was faithful and acceptable? If not, compare your translation to the source language with these questions in mind. If you have any revisions to your translation, write them in the space provided or videotape your corrections if you are working into a signed language.

    _____

    _____

    _____

    _____

2. Circle in blue any parts of the transcript that you had difficulty translating. Circle in red any parts of the transcript whose translation is not equivalent.

3. Examine the translation process to improve the translation product. Refer to the parts of the transcript that you circled in study question 2 and in the areas where your translation is not equivalent,. Write the line numbers of the source message in the space provided and indicate if each error is very serious, quite serious, somewhat serious, or not serious.

    _____

    _____

    _____

    _____

4. For errors marked "very serious" at what stage in the translation process did the difficulty occur?

_____

_____

5. Select one paragraph of your translation and back translate it into written English. Remember that the back translation should be a literal translation. Describe what happens to the meaning when you back translate the passage.

_____

_____

_____

_____

_____

_____

_____

_____

Five-Step Follow-up

Both the translation and the testing of the translation must be completed before you do the follow-up.

Step 1   Observation

Review your translation and your answers to the study questions.

Step 2   Selection

Select the part of the testing process you would most like to improve upon, hypothesis testing or fidelity testing, and select a portion of your translation that contained at least one error. Indicate your selection by circling the corresponding portion of the source text and write the line numbers in the space provided.

_____

_____

_____

_____

Step 3   Analysis

Analyze the error you selected in step 2 and write down the probable cause for the error.

_____

_____

_____

_____

Step 4   Assessment

Once you have decided on a probable cause for the error you selected in step 2 describe the impact of the error on the translation. Was it a serious or not serious error? Did it affect information that came after it?

_____

_____

_____

_____

Step 5   **Action**

Write your plan of action to improve your performance based on what you have discovered about your work in steps 1 through 4.

_____

_____

_____

_____

_____

Progress Tracking Sheet

Use this sheet to track your progress with the exercises you have completed. After performing an exercise (one or two times), answering the study questions, and doing the follow-up, fill in the tracking sheet. Note the date that you completed the exercise and give an indication of your level of accomplishment. You can use either a quantitative or a qualitative approach to track your progress.

Exercise Number	Date	First Performance	Study Questions	Follow-up Activity	Questions and Reminders	Date	Second Performance
Exercise 6.1 Quantitative Qualitative							
Exercise 6.2 Quantitative Qualitative							
Exercise 6.3 Quantitative Qualitative							
Quantitative Totals							

References

The American Heritage Dictionary of the English Language, 3rd Edition. 1992. Boston: Houghton-Mifflin.

Baker, M. (1992). *In other words: A coursebook on translation.* New York: Routledge, Chapman & Hall.

Bell, R. (1991). *Translation and translating: Theory and practice.* New York: Longman.

Boatner, M., and Gates, J. (Eds) (1966). *Dictionary of idioms for the deaf.* West. Hartford, CT: American School for the Deaf.

Catford, J. C. (1965). *A linguistic theory of translation.* London: Oxford University Press.

Chesterman (2000). Teaching strategies for emancipatory translation. In C.Schaffner & B. Adab (Eds.), *Developing translation competence (pp.77–91).* Philadelphia: John Benjamins.

Conference of Interpreter Trainers (1996). *CIT position paper: Instructional class size interpreter training,* 13 (4).

Dreyfus, H. L. & Dreyfus, S. E. (1986). *Mind over machine.* Oxford: Blackwell.

Dollerup, C. (1994). Systematic feedback in teaching translation. In C. Dollerup, & A. Loddegaard (Eds.), *Teaching translation and interpreting, 2* (pp. 121–132). Philadelphia: John Benjamins.

Dollerup, C., & Loddegaard, A. (Eds.) (1992). *Teaching translation and interpreting.* Philadelphia: John Benjamins.

Dollerup, C., & Loddegaard, A. (Eds.) (1994). *Teaching translation and interpreting, 2.* Philadelphia: John Benjamins.

Dollerup, C., & Vibeke, A. (1996). *Teaching translation and interpreting, 3.* Philadelphia: John Benjamins.

Fleetwood, E. (1998). Personal communication.

Fleetwood, E. (2001). Personal communication.

Fillmore, C. (1977). Scenes and frames semantics. Zampolli, Antonio.(Ed.) *Linguistic structures processing*. Amsterdam: North Holland. 55–88.

Fraser, J. (2000). The broader view: How freelance translators define translation competence. In C. Schaffner & B. Adab (Eds.), *Developing translation competence* (pp. 51-62). Philadelphia: John Benjamins.

Gaddis Rose, M. (Ed.) (1987). Editor's note: What translation excellence entails. In *Translation excellence: Assessment, achievement, maintenance.* American Translator's Monograph Series, Vol. 1. Binghamton, NY: University Center at Binghamton.

Gile, D. (1994). The process-oriented approach in translation training: In C. Dollerup & A. Loddegaard (Eds.), Teaching translation and interpreting, 2 (pp.107–112). Philadelphia: John Benjamins.

Gile, D. (1995). *Basic concepts and models for interpreter and translator training.* Philadelphia: John Benjamins.

Gonzalez, R., *et al.* (1991) *Fundamentals in court interpretation: Theory, policy, and practice.* Durham, NC: Carolina Academic Press.

Gorman, D. (1989). Personal communication.

Guilford, J. (1975). Creativity: A quarter century of progress. In I. Taylor & J. Getzels (Eds.), *Perspectives in creativity (pp. 37–59).* Chicago: Aldine.

Kiraly, D. (1990). *Toward a systematic approach to translation skills instruction.* Ann Arbor, MI: University of Michigan.

Kussmaul, P. (1995). *Training the translator.* Philadelphia: John Benjamins.

Landau, E. (1969). *Psychologie der Kreativitat.* Munich: Reinhardt.

Larson, M. (1984). *Meaning based translation: A guide to cross-language equivalence.* Lanham, MD: University of America Press.

Larson, M. (1987). Establishing project specific criteria. In M. Gaddis Rose (Ed.), *Translation excellence: Assessment, achievement, maintenance.* American Translator's Monograph Series, Vol. 1. Binghamtom, NY: University Center at Binghampton.

Lilova, A. (1987). The perfect translation-Ideal and reality. In M. Gaddis Rose (Ed.), *Translation excellence: Assessment, achievement, maintenance.* American Translator's Monograph Series, Vol. 1 (pp 9–18). Binghamton, NY: University Center at Binghamton.

Makkai, A. (Ed.) (1975). *A dictionary of American idioms.* Woodbury, NY: Baron's Educational Series.

Nida, E., & Tabor, C. (1982). *The theory and practice of translation.* Leiden: E. J. Brill.

Neubert, A. (2000). Competence in language, in languages, and in translation. In C. Schaffner & B. Adab (Eds.), *Developing translation competence* (pp. 3–19). Philadelphia: John Benjamins.

Nord, C. (1995). Teaching translation without languages? Some considerations on the structural aspects of translator training. In A. Neubert, G. Shreve, & K. Gommlich (Eds.), *Basic issues in translation studies (pp. 283–291).* Kent: Kent State University Press.

"Ptolemy V," Microsoft Encarta® Online Encyclopedia 2001 http://encarta.msn.com © 1997-2001 Microsoft.

Roberts, R. (1994) Student competencies in interpreting: Defining teaching and evaluating. In E.A. Winston (Ed.) *Mapping our course: A collaborative venture.* Proceedings of the 10th National Convention, Conference of Interpreter Trainers. Charlotte, NC.

Schaffner, C., & Adab, B. (Eds.) (2000). *Developing translation competence.* Philadelphia: John Benjamins

Seal, B. (1999). Educational interpreters document efforts to improve. *VIEWS,* 16(2), p. 14. Silver Spring, MD: Registry for Interpreters for the Deaf.

Seleskovich, D., & Lederer, M. (1989). *A systematic approach to teaching interpretation.* Silver Spring, MD: Registry for Interpreters for the Deaf.

Snell-Hornby, M. (1995). *Translation studies: An integrated approach.* Philadelphia: John Benjamins.

Snell-Hornby, M., *et al.* (Eds.) (1992). *Translation studies: An interdiscipline.* Philadelphia: John Benjamins

Vermeer, H. (1989). Skopos and commission in translational action. In A. Chesterman (Ed.) *Empirical research in translation and intercultural studies (pp. 79–88).* Tubingen:Narr.

Widdowson, H. G. (1978). *Teaching language as communication.* London: Oxford University Press.